Twayne's English Authors Series

EDITOR OF THIS VOLUME

Kinley E. Roby

Northeastern University

Paul Scott

TEAS 285

Paul Scott

PAUL SCOTT

By K. BHASKARA RAO

University of Nevada, Reno

TWAYNE PUBLISHERS
A DIVISION OF G. K. HALL & CO., BOSTON

Published in 1980 by Twayne Publishers,
A Division of G. K. Hall & Co.
All Rights Reserved

Printed on permanent/durable acid-free paper and bound
in the United States of America

First Printing

Frontispiece photo of Paul Scott © by Mark Gerson

Library of Congress Cataloging in Publication Data
Rao, Kanatur Bhaskara, 1926–
Paul Scott.

(Twayne's English authors series; TEAS 285)
Bibliography: p. 157–64
Includes index.
1. Scott, Paul, 1920–1978
—Criticism and interpretation.
PR6069.C596Z85   823′.914   80–422
ISBN 0-8057-6773-8

To the memory of my parents
Indiramma and Hanumantha Rao

Contents

About the Author

K. Bhaskara Rao is Advisor and Counselor to International Students at the University of Nevada, Reno. He was educated at the Universities of Mysore and Nagpur in India and received his doctorate from the University of Iowa. He has served as Executive Director of World University Service, New York, and in that capacity visited and lectured at more than six hundred colleges and universities both in the U.S. and overseas. He was also Director of the American Language Program, Nasson College, Maine. Dr. Rao is the author of two novels: *Yachts, Hamburgers and A Hindu; Candle Against the Wind*; two Plays: *Gandhi* (which won the first prize at the International Playwriting Contest sponsored by Southern Illinois University); *A Gathering of Beggars*; and a critical study, *Rudyard Kipling's India*. He has also served as editor of *The New Quarterly*, a journal devoted to creative writing about Asia. Dr. Rao's areas of specialization includes the literature of imperialism and intercultural interpretations in contemporary fiction. He is a member of the American PEN Center and the Dramatists Guild, New York. He is currently working on a book, *Global Education and the Humanities: The Imperative Partnership*.

Preface

The rise and fall of the British Empire, the biggest theme open to British writers, was Paul Scott's milieu. In nine novels and a four-novel sequence, *The Raj Quartet*, Scott examined, scrutinized, and laid bare from a variety of perspectives the manifold aspects of the British experience in India. Within a thoroughly researched historical framework, Scott created a world of his own in which he dramatized the interpersonal relations of men and women with different cultural and racial backgrounds.

The present study of Paul Scott as a novelist is the result of my personal conviction that (1) Paul Scott is a major novelist of the twentieth century; (2) that his major work, *The Raj Quartet*, because of its intense moral tone and humanistic interpretation of interpersonal, intercultural relations, is not only a masterpiece of British literature but of world literature; (3) that it can be favorably compared and ranked with Tolstoy's *War and Peace* and Ford Madox Ford's Christopher Tietjens tetralogy, *Parade's End*. I have discussed Scott's place and rank more fully in the concluding chapter of this study.

My purpose in this study is to provide an introduction to Scott's novels as a whole, and to encourage his reading and study by a wider audience.

It was a temptation to begin the study with *The Raj Quartet*, but since Scott's writings reflect both his development as a novelist and his preparation for his masterpiece, I have approached the study from a chronological and thematic perspective. In my analysis of the novels, I have emphasized his distinctive narrative techniques, the development of prominent themes, and the portrayal of complex and varied characters. I have included in the study of each novel a brief but coherent plot summary to assist the reader.

This is the first full-length study of Paul Scott. There is little critical writing except for reviews of his novels in journals and newspapers, and I have incorporated these in my discussion.

Paul Scott had known that this book was being written. He was generous with his time and granted me two interviews. The first one lasted little more than four hours and ranged over a wide variety of topics. The second interview, which took place about four months later, had to be terminated after half an hour, because Scott was physically and emotionally exhausted. I have drawn upon these interviews in the course of this study.

Chapter 1 deals with the principal facts of Scott's life. The second chapter discusses his early attempts at poetry and the publication of his first novel, *Johnnie Sahib*. Scott's two English novels are discussed in the third chapter. Since *The Corrida at San Feliu* has autobiographical overtones, particularly in expressing Scott's personal views on the art of writing the novel, a separate chapter has been devoted to its analysis. Chapter 5 discusses themes and techniques in the four novels in which Scott was "warming up" to write the major work of his career, *The Raj Quartet*. I have devoted four chapters to the study of *The Raj Quartet*: as story; as history; as a study in race and class; and as a novel. I have by no means exhausted the study of *The Raj Quartet* and have suggested, in the course of my discussion, other possible themes that deserve further study. The work can be mined endlessly, which is one of its major strengths. *Staying On*, Scott's last novel, follows the lives of two minor characters from *The Raj Quartet*, Tusker and Lucy. Because of its terminal tone and comic style, I have devoted an entire chapter to its discussion.

I am thankful to Mr. John Willey, Scott's American editor at William Morrow and Co.; Mrs. Dorothy Olding, Scott's Literary Agent, Harold Ober and Co., New York; and Mr. Ronald Gant, Editorial Director, William Heinemann, London, for their time and assistance in answering questions. I am thankful to Mr. Peter B. Scott for providing me with a copy of Scott's poem *Charing Cross Station*.

All references to Scott's novels are to the American editions, for which permission has been kindly granted by William Morrow and Co. References to *The Raj Quartet* are to the one-volume edition. References to *Johnnie Sahib* and *The Mark of the Warrior* are from the English editions, and permission to quote from them has been obtained by William Heinemann. Permission to quote from T. S. Eliot's *East Coker* has been obtained by Harcourt Brace Jovanovich, New York.

Scott's manuscripts are on deposit at the Humanities Research Center, University of Texas, Austin.

K. Bhaskara Rao

University of Nevada, Reno

Chronology

1920   Paul Mark Scott born March 25, Fox Lane, Palmer's Green, a suburb of London; one of two sons of Tom and Frances Scott.

1929–   Early education at Winchmore Hill Collegiate School, a
1935   private school in London.

1936   Trains with the accounting firm of C. T. Payne in London. Attends evening classes in accountancy. Spends leisure time writing poetry.

1940   Joins British Army Brigade Intelligence as a noncommissioned officer.

1941   Marries Nancy E. Avery. *I, Gerontius—A Trilogy*, a poem in the Resurgam Younger Poets Series.

1942   Leaves British Army Brigade Intelligence.

1943   June, first visit to India as officer cadet. Works as air supply specialist. Travels extensively on the subcontinent with side trips to Imphal and Malaya.

1946   Returns to Britain after the war. Works as accountant and later as company secretary for the Falcon-Greywalls Press in London, a firm owned and run by the late Peter Baker, Labor M.P. in association with Charles Wray Gardiner, writer and editor of *Poetry Quarterly*.

1947   Birth of daughter, Carol Vivien.

1948   Birth of second daughter, Sally Elizabeth. *Pillars of Salt* (play).

1950   Leaves Falcon-Greywalls Press; joins Pearn Pollinger and Higham (Later David Higham Associates) as literary agent.

1951   Wins the Eyre and Spottiswoode Literary Award for *Johnnie Sahib*.

1952   *Johnnie Sahib*

1953   *Johnnie Sahib* adapted for BBC radio and television as *Lines of Communication*. *The Alien Sky*, published as *Six Days in Marapore* in America.

1955   *Sahibs and Memsahibs*: a radio play produced by Archie Campbell on BBC.

1956   *A Male Child.*

1958   *The Mark of the Warrior.* Visits Spain for the first time, makes it an annual visit through 1963.

1960   Leaves Higham's to write full time. *The Chinese Love Pavilion*, published as *The Love Pavilion* in America.

1962   *The Birds of Paradise.*

1963   Elected Fellow of the Royal Society of Literature. *The Bender.*

1964   *The Corrida at San Feliu.* Makes return trip to India, financed by Heinemann publishers. Stays with middle-class professional Indian families. Begins work on *The Raj Quartet.*

1966   *The Jewel in the Crown.*

1968   *The Day of the Scorpion.* Delivers lecture, *India—A Post Forsterian View*, to the *Royal Society of Literature.* Heinemann publishes Collected Edition of Scott's novels.

1969   Makes third trip to India. Receives Arts Council Grant.

1971   *The Towers of Silence.* Wins the *Yorkshire Post* Fiction Award.

1972   Makes fourth and last visit to India for the British Council in connection with the International Book Year. Addresses various universities and literary gatherings throughout the country.

1975   Concludes *The Raj Quartet* with the publication of *A Division Of The Spoils.* Visits the United States. Lectures and reads passages from *The Raj Quartet* to audiences at universities and colleges in Washington, D.C., Maryland, Texas, Illinois, and New York.

1976   Serves as writer in residence at the Institute of Modern Letters, University of Tulsa, Oklahoma. Offers a seminar on *The Exotic Heresy and the Insular Tradition.*

1977   Returns to Tulsa for teaching. *Staying On* wins England's highest literary award, the Booker Award. *The Raj Quartet* published in one volume. Enters hospital in Tulsa. While recuperating begins work on a new novel.

1978   March 1, dies of cancer in Middlesex Hospital, London.

CHAPTER 1

Paul Scott: A Biographical Note

ON hearing the news of Paul Scott's death, on March 1, 1978, John Leonard of the *New York Times*—who lived for months in Scott's mind, and called it "a very civilised place to be"[1]—uttered the appropriate epitaph: "He advertised nothing of himself. He merely wrote fine books."[2]

For over a quarter of a century, carefully, conscientiously, unhurriedly, Paul Scott had devoted himself to "the most exacting form of writing, there is," that of the novel.[3] He took his profession seriously, devoutly. It was his burnt offering, and he would have agreed with Malcolm Cowley's description of the act of writing as a priestly vocation with its own ethical code. Scott kept himself aloof from "the metropolitan literary lunatic asylum"[4] of London and over a lifetime patiently built up an impressive oeuvre, thereby making his contribution to literature permanent. While he was aware that in modern times "those whose work is best publicised are those who are themselves the best publicists, rather than those who tell the most riveting tales,"[5] he did not succumb to the temptation of the quick success, the flashy and the trendy, but patiently went about his task of writing, devoting ten years to completing his masterpiece, *The Raj Quartet.*

I *Work Habits*

Scott was at his place of writing, day in and day out, to patiently wait on the muse, to use a Jamesian expression. Scott was fond of quoting Raymond Chandler, the American mystery writer, who believed that all writing that had any life in it was done with the solar plexus; that it was exhausting; that a professional writer set aside a period of time when he did nothing else, because, "A. You don't have to write. B. You can't do anything else. The rest comes of itself."[6]

Scott wrote in longhand, preferring the quiet of pen and paper, for his first expression. The following morning he would type up what he had written the night before. This would make him get back into the book and reset the stage for him to start again. Often he would stop writing in the middle of a sentence, knowing how it would end. This mid-sentence stop would be like a thread to follow either forward or backward.

II   *"The work is all that matters"*

In a letter to the author of this study, Scott wrote, "There isn't much biographical stuff on record at the moment. I've always kept it at a minimum, since it has generally seemed to me to be irrelevant to the work itself. On top of which there's this inclination every novelist must have to nurse his autobiography, knowing it might be the last novel he ever writes."[7]

Like Edward Thornhill, the fictional novelist in the novel *The Corrida at San Feliu*, Scott believed "the work is all that matters."[8]

III   *Birth, Parentage, and Education*

Paul Mark Scott was born in Palmers Green, a suburb of London, on March 25, 1920. He was the second of two sons in a family of self-employed commercial artists. His mother elegantly modeled lavish furs, which she could not afford to own, and his father painted them attractively for catalogs of wholesale furriers. His mother also wrote novels, secretively, prior to her marriage in 1916. But the night of her wedding she is supposed to have burned all the manuscripts and only remembered the title of her favorite novel: *The Keepsake*. Paul Scott was not certain about his mother's ventures in novel writing, but credited her with a vivid imagination, and believed he had inherited this talent from her.

Scott's two uncles, George and Gilbert (actually they were his father's close cousins) were also commercial artists. Their paintings, mostly horses and hunting scenes, still crop up at Sotheby's and Christies for auction. The Scotts were supposed to be connected with the eighteenth-century naturalist and engraver Thomas Bewick, and Bewick has been used as a middle name for male Scotts for the eldest boy for a long time, as in the case of Paul Scott's older brother, Peter Bewick Scott.

Scott spent his childhood and youth in Palmers Green and in the neighboring district of Southgate. He too had wanted to follow the family line and become an artist. But he discovered that he could not meet the high standards set by his family. He also experienced happiness and greater facility in the use of words rather than in the use of paints and brush. To add to this decision, not to pursue a career as a commercial artist, was his mother's insistence that someone in the family not be poor, and so Scott's father directed him to choosing a monetarily safe career, that of an accountant.

Although mathematics was Scott's weakest subject, he had a photographic memory which enabled him to pass exams with supreme ease. Thus, after an early education at Winchmore Hill Collegiate School, described as a private school for sons of gentlemen, from which Scott did not matriculate, he was placed with a firm of accountants in London to learn the profession at the age of sixteen. Because he had not matriculated, Scott had to take a full range of academic subjects in order to take the preliminary accountancy exam, which he did two years later when he reached eighteen, the earliest age permitted to take it. He passed the exams gloriously, and while he was preparing himself to take the next higher accountancy exams, scheduled for 1941, the war interrupted his plans and he was drafted. He abandoned his plans to become a professional accountant.

This was just as well. "Often when I should have been thinking about the Law of Contract, or the Laws relating to Bankruptcy and Receivership, or the Principles of Auditing or Economics, I was writing verse and plays and planning to write a novel."[9]

IV *Army and India*

After being drafted into the British army, he stayed for two years as a noncommissioned officer in brigade intelligence and was then shipped to India as a sergeant in the British Indian Army. He arrived in India in 1943, one year after the major confrontation—a turning point in the fortunes of the Raj—between Indians and British had taken place over the 1942 British Quit India resolution. This catalytic event was in the years to come to provide the backdrop for Scott's major work, *The Raj Quartet.*

Paul Scott was a raw amateur when he first arrived in India. He was totally ignorant about the subcontinent. He had not questioned the choice made for him, because he thought India would be a warmer place and hence better there than in the damp and cold of England. There was no one in Scott's family connected with India, except possibly a distant aunt whose husband had built bridges there at one time. There were no Raj connections, and neither had Scott been brought up on Kipling, the standard fare of young English children, "because he couldn't bear talking animals."[10] He had of course heard of such clichés as the Black Hole of Calcutta, the heat and humidity of the land, and its terrible backwardness and poverty. The monsoon rains were in full force and fury when he arrived in India, and Scott promptly jaundiced with a bad case of hepatitis. He hated the land and regretted his coming.

But as officer cadet attached to the airsupply unit, Scott was able to crisscross the vast land with side trips to Imphal and Malaya. Three years in India cast a hypnotic spell over him. Its vastness; its sense of mystery; the sharp contrasts of incredible beauty side by side with the faces of damnation; fabulous wealth and stark poverty, repelled and fascinated him. India took possession of him, challenging his mind and imagination. He formed a gradual attachment to the land and its people, and India became his spiritual home.

After the war came an obsession for India. The land quickened his pulse, released his creativity, and resulted in his many novels culminating in *The Raj Quartet*. Of his ten novels (*The Raj Quartet* is considered as one novel) only three did not *specifically* have an Indian setting, and even these three are sprinkled generously with references from Scott's Indian experience. He was to say, "My India made me talkative, Forster's stunned him into silence."[11]

V   *Company Secretary and Literary Agent*

Returning to England in 1946 and following demobilization, Scott used his knowledge of accountancy to obtain a job as company secretary to a Janus-headed publishing house—the Falcon and Greywalls Press.[12] Although the firm imported such American writers as Tennessee Williams, F. Scott Fitzgerald, and Nathanael West, Scott was soon to discover the unethical nature of the enterprise. Protests of impatient creditors grew louder and getting the monthly check more hazardous, so Scott quit in 1950, and the firm went bankrupt soon after. Scott then joined the firm of Pearn, Pollinger and Higham as a literary agent. He liked his job, which gave him an opportunity to satisfy, at least vicariously, his own hunger to be a writer. He gave equal attention to every writer he handled whether the author was a writer of a literary work or pure escapist fiction—a murder mystery or a gothic romance. A best-selling author and a poor seller both got equal treatment, a point on which some of his associates became a bit sensitive. Among Scott's clients were Muriel Spark, Morris West, James Leasor, Francis Clifford, and Roland Gant. Knowledge of his accountancy also helped, for as an agent Scott had to add up the profits and percentages of his clients!

As a literary agent Scott continued to nurse his private dream of becoming a full-time writer, someday. He wrote poetry, plays, and novels. He destroyed his first novel. His second novel *Johnnie Sahib*, after being turned down by seventeen publishers, finally got published in 1952. It won an award and went on to become a successful radio play. However, it was not until 1960, when he was forty years old, that Scott gave up his literary agency career to devote full time to being a writer.

VI *Return to India and* The Raj Quartet

After his early three-year army career in India, Scott had not revisited the subcontinent for eighteen years. During this period he continued to work under the Indian spell by studying Indian history and drawing upon his Indian experience to write eight novels.

While the Anglo-Indian world of the British Raj was remote and getting even farther away, the place and period of Anglo-India continued to exert great interest for Scott. He saw in it what Michael Edwards, a prolific British historian of Anglo-India had seen, namely, India as a laboratory for English social experiment. Scott saw in it a metaphor for the English pursuit of happiness at home.[13]

In order to take another look at "the larger left-over portion of the laboratory"[14] Scott returned to India in 1964. The trip was financed by Heinemann, his publishers, to recharge his batteries, but with no pressure or commitment to produce anything.[15]

The trip proved extremely rewarding. Scott stayed with middle-class Indian families,[16] renewed acquaintances, and traveled extensively. Out of this and subsequent visits in 1969 and 1972 was fashioned the sequence of four novels that make up *The Raj Quartet*.

VII *Review Work, Teaching, and Death*

Scott was a prolific reviewer of books for *Country Life* magazine, *The Daily Telegraph*, and occasionally for the London *Times*.[17] He selected the books he reviewed, choosing biographies and history over fiction. Review work gave him an opportunity to read books that he normally would not have read.

He gave to these reviews the same careful and meticulous attention he gave to his novels, balancing his judgments, weighing his comments, and bringing to bear upon his critical opinion, the wealth of his reading and experience.

The completion of *The Raj Quartet* in 1975 and its subsequent publication in one volume, brought belated but deserved recognition of Scott's superb talents as a major novelist.

In the fall of 1975 he visited the United States and lectured at various universities and read with dramatic effect passages from *The Raj Quartet.*

He had already begun work on yet another novel, inspired by two walk-on characters from *The Raj Quartet.* Titled *Staying On*, the novel comically and poignantly portrayed the lives of two survivors from the days of the Raj, who had opted to stay on in independent India. It turned out to be Scott's last novel.

In the fall of 1976, Scott returned to the United States as visiting professor and writer in residence at the University of Tulsa, Oklahoma. He offered a seminar on *The Exotic Heresy and the Insular Tradition* and also offered a course on creative writing. Teaching was a new experience for him, but he prepared for his classes with the same seriousness he gave to his writing. His impact on his students and his ability to communicate with them proved so effective, that Scott was reinvited by the University of Tulsa for the fall of 1977.

His second teaching assignment was interrupted by his illness and he was operated upon for cancer. While recuperating and thinking about his next novel, Scott learned that *Staying On* had won England's coveted Booker Award for the best work of fiction published in 1977.

Scott returned to England in December 1977 feeling optimistic about his health. There was a note of tranquillity and contentment in one of his last letters to the author of this study.[18]

Tragically, "while poised on the rim of something like widespread popularity,"[19] Scott had to be operated upon again and died on March 1, 1978, at the age of fifty-seven.

VIII   *His Philosophic Credo*

Scott admired T. S. Eliot, was fond of quoting from him extensively, and had often stated that the concluding lines from Eliot's *East Coker* admirably stated his own philosophic credo. We can do no better than repeat those lines:

Old men ought to be explorers
Here and there does not matter
We must be still and still moving.
Into another intensity
For a further union, a deeper communion
Through the dark cold and the empty desolation,
The wave cry, the wind cry, the vast waters
Of the petrel and the porpoise. In my end is my beginning.[20]

CHAPTER 2

Early Writings:
Poetry, Plays, and a Novel

I *Poetry*

AS a young man, Scott indulged himself in writing poetry for self expression and dreamed of becoming a poet in the tradition of Auden, Spender, and Eliot. But he met with little success in terms of publication and abandoned the goal of becoming a poet. Even though he gave up writing poetry, it continued to be one of his literary passions throughout his life: he retained the poet's respect for words and remained acutely conscious of their meticulous and precise usage. When he lectured and reviewed books, he always found an opportunity to quote the appropriate passages from other poets to illustrate and strengthen his ideas. In *The Raj Quartet* Scott created the fictional Urdu poet Gaffur and his poetry, and thus incorporated into his major work his first love, that of writing poetry.

Only two of his poems survive for our brief examination: *I, Gerontius*, published in 1941 and "Charing Cross Station" an unpublished poem written on July 28, 1941.

I, Gerontius[1], written as a trilogy and divided into three sections, the Creation, the Dream, and the Cross, is an impressionistic poem with imagery drawn from the Bible. It expresses a young man's feelings before he enters the army and affirms the need for a strong religious belief, for "Everlasting Life."

"Charing Cross Station"[2] is about the artificiality of modern life with its routine clichés about pretentious human relations and the deadening of human sensibilities brought upon by the horrors of war. There is a brittle, cynical feeling of nihilistic despair throughout the poem. This feeling and lines such as "Holding the last pathetic cup of coffee amidst the light oak and gleaming bottles of a buffet" and "Like dry seeds in old earth," are clear attempts by Scott to echo and imitate T. S. Eliot.

II *Plays*

Scott wrote four radio plays. Two of these were adapted from his novels *The Alien Sky* and *The Mark of the Warrior*. Since these scripts are unavailable, they cannot be reviewed in any detail.

Of the two original radio plays, "Pillars of Salt" (which is amateurish and melodramatic with a stilted plot involving an episode in the army) and "Sahibs and Memsahibs",[3] only the latter is worth consideration.

"Sahibs and Memsahibs" is set in India. The year is 1943 and the locale is a military cantonment, like Marapore in *The Alien Sky*, and the plot revolves around the two Memsahibs in their attempts to outwit each other. Mrs. Gore, wife of the colonel, self-appointed arbiter of the social code, is a stuffy pompous lady, jealous of Mrs. Nan Forrest's popularity with the young cadets. Mrs. Forrest, an iconoclast, a divorcee, resides at Smith's Hotel and treats the cadets to coffee and sympathy, interspersed with Urdu lessons and helpful short-cut hints to assist them in passing their military exams. They adore her and feel like human beings in her company. To Mrs. Gore all these activities spell sinful flirtation and lack of proper conduct.

Since Mrs. Forrest cannot be punished, the cadets are threatened with the prospect of losing their commission in good regiments. Mrs. Forrest loves the cadets, so she sets about trying to save them from such a disaster. Mrs. Gore and Mrs. Forrest plot and counterplot, and in the end Mrs. Forrest outwits Mrs. Gore.

The play successfully presents the tight knit, class-conscious world of the British in India, a world that Scott was to open up for minute scrutiny in his later novels.

Although Scott did not write a stage play, which he very much wanted to,[4] his feel for the theater sharpened and developed within the scope of the novel, the literary form he mastered. His ability to set a stage, light a scene, introduce and develop character out of action and dialogue is demonstrated repeatedly in some of his novels. In *The Bender* and *The Raj Quartet*, as we will see later, there are episodes which lend themselves to effective stage presentations. Scott's theatrical interests greatly aided him as a novelist.

III Johnnie Sahib

Scott wrote two novels as part of his early apprenticeship. The first novel, "is fortunately not in existence."[5] Farley Morley, brother of

Christopher Morley (*Kitty Foyle*), was the only other person besides Scott who had seen this work, and told Scott, "Paul, you are not going to write anymore like this."[6] It was both a question and a command, with emphasis on the command. The next novel he wrote was *Johnnie Sahib*.

Scott collected seventeen rejection slips for *Johnnie Sahib* before he found a publisher. Of this early rejection, Scott was to say, "Writers must have failures early in their careers. It sorts out those who go on. You need a lot of stamina."[7] When *Johnnie Sahib* was finally published, it won the coveted Eyre and Spottiswoode Literary Award and was later adapted successfully for a BBC radio play by Donald McWhinnie under the title "Lines of Communication." Ian Watkins produced it on television as well.

Johnnie Sahib concerns itself with "the difficulty of one officer (Jim Taylor) in India during the war taking over another officer's (Johnnie Sahib) job."[8] Thus in his very first published novel, Scott indicates the central metaphor—man defined in relationship to his job—of all his later novels.

The Japanese have crossed the border between Burma and India, posing an imminent threat to invade Kohima and Imphal. It was during this campaign that for the first time, air transport was effectively used to penetrate enemy lines by dropping supplies, hauling out the wounded, and reconnoitering. The traditional ground lines of communication were extended, and thus a major breakthrough achieved in military strategy, proving that "an army can move with the air as its only line of communication." (1).

Twenty-five-year-old Johnnie Brown is a member of this air transportation unit. He is part of this new "lines of communication," but in a larger sense he also has effective lines of communication with his team mates and therein lies his strength.

He is also a member of the white race, of the ruling class in India and thus automatically heir to a position of power and authority. In England, as a member of the lower middle class, Johnnie would have been denied such privileges. The prestige and authority an Englishman enjoyed in India by the mere fact of being white, a mark of superiority and infallibility, was incredible.

Johnnie's attitude toward his Indian crew members is a paternalistic attitude; they are simple and innocent and so need to be punished and protected. He knows all their names, their strengths, and their weaknesses, and inspires in them unity, coordination, and comradeship. He has hand picked each and every one of them, and stands up for them "against the least threat of outside influence" (6). The men respond with their unswerving loyalty.

The heart of the novel is a confrontation between Johnnie, the individualist who refuses to fit into the army pattern, and the old major who goes strictly by the book. The major wants to break Johnnie, and fit him into the mold of army life. The major uses Johnnie's vacation as an opportunity to reshape Johnnie's section by giving it over to another officer, Jim Taylor.

Jim Taylor has also come under the spell of Johnnie. In his obsession to make himself a hero to Johnnie's men, Jim Taylor makes a mistake, a simple error of a lesser load of ammunition on a plane than the required amount. But he covers up his mistake at the suggestion of one of his Indian crew members. It is his way of showing that he trusts and values the opinion of his Indian crew. But even as he enters into this conspiracy of a coverup, he realizes that, "he was being controlled, directed, used. Used as one is used by others and blackmailed into a lie with continued, grudging favor as the lie's reward" (11).

The major is aware of this coverup and uses it to blame and break Johnnie when he returns, pointing out that when one ignores the time honored military rules and regulation, corruption of an institution by coverup is the result. The major deprives Johnnie of his section because that is *the* only thing that would hurt him (12).

Johnnie goes to another post in Ambala but his men miss him, and their thoughts and action are still guided by him.

Exorcising this ghost of Johnnie becomes an obsession with Jim Taylor. Jim who had begun his job emulating Johnnie, now wants to get rid of Johnnie "who's like a ghost at his elbow" (15). Jim wants Johnnie's section to become his section, total and complete. He does not succeed in achieving such a transformation. Jim orders a risky airlift of petrol and rations behind enemy lines, to show his skills in planning and commanding a military operation. But the plane crashes and an Indian orderly, Jan Mohammed, is burned to death in the flames. Thus tragically, Jim Taylor realizes and confesses to Johnnie in a letter, "I can't attempt to hold on any longer to what doesn't belong to me and never belonged to me" (16).

Johnnie Brown and Jim Taylor are the only two sharply defined characters in the novel. The Indian characters for the most part are orderlies and servants, except for Johns, the Anglo-Indian of mixed race. Johns is a pathetic figure as he heroically attempts to pass himself off for an Englishman, "pretending to a childhood in

Buckinghamshire. He had never been further west than Bombay, but from books and talking to others Johns had formed for himself a vision of England and at the last convinced himself he had been there; for it was a confession of mixed blood not to have been 'home'" (18).

Although *Johnnie Sahib* won an award and gave Scott his entry into the publishing world, in later years he was clearly embarrassed by it. He called it "bloody awful"[9] and in a letter to the author of this study said, "It's not a good book, so you wouldn't be missing much."[10] But Scott believed that an author must be judged by his total work, good and bad, and as for *Johnnie Sahib*, "There are three things you can do with a first book: Suppress it, rewrite it or admit it. I admit Johnnie, because the faults are not his, they are mine."[11]

CHAPTER 3

The English Novels

O F Scott's ten novels, *A Male Child* (1956), his third novel, and *The Bender* (1963), his seventh novel, have an English setting. But echoes of India are heard in both of them, and there is an expression of wistful nostalgia for the loss of the Empire resulting in the shrinking of opportunities for an Englishman.

"There's no scope for a man any more," complains a character in *A Male Child*, reflecting on the old days when a young man was able to make something of himself by going East: "We've won the war and lost the Empire in the process" (185). Ian Canning, the central character in the novel, realizes that wherever he went in England and whatever he talked about, he was always conscious of his "Indian days" and that "there was no escaping them" (105). He had gone to India in 1942, the critical year for the British because of the "Quit India" resolution, and he is reflecting on India in 1947, with the dissolution of the Empire but a few months away.

In *The Bender*, too, there is a similar realization that it was India, England's Eastern Empire, that had made "the English middle class" (31). No longer can young men succumb "to the lure of the poor man's Disraeli, Mr. Rudyard Kipling," and go "East of Suez" (57) in search of new opportunities.

There are other similarities in the two English novels. Ian in *A Male Child*, and George in *The Bender*, each have a legacy, however small it is, and hence are robbed of the vital hunger to find a job that would maximize their full capabilities. Therefore they drift, George going on benders and Ian looking for a home or family to attach himself to, neither one knowing precisely what one wants out of life. In them Scott finds his metaphor of man in relationship to his job.

Both George and Ian are childless, and cannot have "heirs." Ian takes a vicarious pleasure in his friend Alan's male child, while George gets his satisfaction by being close to his goddaughter Gillian's child. Both novels conclude on the birth of a child, on a note of hope.

The novels also indicate certain themes which Scott was to develop more fully in his later novels. The period of 1942–1947, the time span in *A Male Child*, was to become the period minutely examined in Scott's major work, *The Raj Quartet*. The sad comedy of *The Bender* and the unpalatable truth, "like the truth of being old and tired" (118), was to find fuller and deeper expression in his last novel *Staying On*.

I A Male Child

A Male Child, Scott's third novel, is "about a man home in London from the war in the East, too ill from tropical infection to do a proper job and feel he had a stake in the future."[1]

Told in the first person, *A Male Child* is the story of Ian Canning who returns to England in 1946 after a four year stay in India, where as Officer Cadet Canning he had "enjoyed being a soldier" (11). He has contracted in India an undiagnosable tropical disease which flares up at intervals. After several medical examinations, his illness is finally diagnosed in Edinburgh and given a tongue twisting medical term for which there is no present cure, but considerable research for a future remedy. David Holmes, a friend, suggests that Ian fight this disease on its own ground by returning to India. Holmes has a selfish interest in Ian's return to India, for then he and his girl friend Peggy can hang on to Ian's flat, hard to come by in postwar England.

But Canning stays in London, and *A Male Child* is essentially his story and his relationships with a host of odd-ball but fascinating characters.

There is his wife Helen, a novelist, who greets Canning upon his return to London by a letter, hard, brittle, and cynical, asking him for divorce. She even provides him with grounds for such action: "I've had another 'miscarriage,' only this time it happened naturally. . . . Boy or girl, it would have melted to jelly by radiation in the next war. This other child would have been Bobbie's and I imagine I couldn't give you more substantial grounds for divorcing me" (15). Ian later learns that "miscarriage" was Helen's word for abortion.

Ian visits Brian Selby, the publisher, with his "ageless face of a somewhat startled baby" (21) for whom Ian had once worked as a reader. Selby offers Ian some part time work as a reader of manuscripts and as his first assignment lends him a copy of an out of print novel, *Opal* by Isabella, first published by the Selby House in 1921. Ian reads it and sends in a negative report.

His next call is on his godfather Commander Owen in Wendover, in the country. Collecting butterflies and fulfilling a parental role, "less for Ian's sake than for his dead parents who he admired" (18), Commander Owen wants to leave his house to Ian, and wants him to make it his headquarters. What Ian really needs is "the vital spark of reaction of people and surroundings," which is not to be found in the commander's house.

Ian next runs into Alan Hurst, his one time army friend from his India days. Alan wants to return to India to plant tea because the image such a possibility conjures up is attractive. "The pipe, the end of the day. The sundowner" (39). But in reality Alan is training for the safe occupation of an accountant. Alan invites Ian to provide him a bit of company, because his wife Stella is away at Aylward, his home.

But Aylward, which once used to be a pleasant place where people "learned a great deal about give and take, more than a normal family" (63), is at present far from normal. Aylward has now fallen upon decadent times, and upon first sight Alan is shocked by "its ugliness, its tall, rectangular nastiness" (43). It is now a series of little flats rented out to nondescript little people. That portion of Aylward, the maisonette, not made into flats is presided over by Alan's alcoholic mother Mrs. Marion Hurst.

Marion Hurst, with her small wasted body, but with a rich, vibrant voice and flamboyant red-dyed hair, is living in a twilight world of delusion and grandeur. She settles down to a long chat with Ian. She pulls out, one by one, the skeletons from the family cupboard. She uninhibitedly pours out her love for her dead first son Edward, a posthumously published poet "Bitter Spring and Other Poems". She is caustic and derogatory about her second son, Alan, friend of Ian. She tells Ian that Alan's wife Stella has left him; that Stella was actually Edward's girl friend. She is equally biting in her scorn of Rex Coles, her brother-in-law husband of novelist Isabella. He is a parasite living off of Isabella's writings.

Marion Hurst shows family photographs to Ian and points out how Rex Coles's daughter Adela Coles (by his first wife), a bohemian witty-shocker type, has a taste for young men and how she had seduced Alan at the tender age of eighteen. Then she launches into the realm of the occult by telling Ian about Mrs. Voremburg, a German lady, who had conjured up the spirit of her dead son Edward. His death of course was the end of the world to her, the death of Aylward as well.

In Ian, Marion sees a likeness of her son Edward, not just

physically, but even mentally, by pointing out that Ian's report to Selby about Isabella's novel "Opal" was similar to the comments Edward had made. Such a comparison makes Ian restless, but gives him "a strange excitement" (77).

Gradually Marion Hurst steers the conversation to fit in with her scheme, to encourage Ian to fulfill her dead son's intention: to write the biography of novelist Isabella. Edward's intention? Was his intention to become my duty? Canning reflects (80).

Marion is persistent. She probes, cajoles, and coaxes Canning to seriously consider the possibility of undertaking Isabella's biography. "It will be at once a pleasure for us and a practical form of convalescence for you," she urges Ian and promises full family cooperation and assistance.

Ian is intrigued but undecided about the writing project. In his reflections on the possibilities of approaching Isabella's biography, we get interesting insights into the mind of a writer. He does not see Isabella as the centerpiece of a book, but as the centerpiece of a portrait of the family, a sort of a link between the Edwardian era and the 1920s. An essay in nostalgia, rather an analysis of the pretentious respectability beneath the real aura of tragedy. And dead Isabella, like Edward, exerts a powerful force on the action in *A Male Child*. It is her novels, "comically old fashioned" and "popular in a middle-brow sort of way" (29), with one word titles, mostly the name of jewels— "Pearl," "Ruby," "Opal"—that kept Rex Coles and Aylward in the black. According to Marion Hurst, Isabella was a great talent, and the story of her life would make a fascinating biography. But Adela Coles thinks of her as "the worst possible sort of literary hack. Sh e was colorless from the day she was born until the day she died" (107). And according to Edward, the only book anyone could write about Isabella would be a novel with her in it as a minor character (113). Even Rex Coles, who at first had supported the idea of Isabella's biography, now wants to prevent it, "poor Isabel. She was a saint, old man. We ought to leave her in peace" (146). He is secretly afraid that her biography would speak of him in words of truth too hard for him to bear.

Ian continues to stay at Aylward even though it is a "nut house" (136). The news of Alan's wife Stella's plan to return tenses Marion Hurst, who begins to seek even greater refuge in the bottle. Alan trembles at the prospect of his mother and wife tearing at each other over infinite trivia. He asks Ian to stay and act as a buffer between his mother and his wife. Lacking a family of any sort and hungering for one, monsters, nuthouse, and all, Ian accepts the responsibility because he sees in "all the people who came and went, in and out of the rooms at Aylward: the human condition of which he is part and parcel" (137). Stella returns, pregnant with Alan's child, a match for Marion. Ian has his hands full to help maintain a cease-fire between the two, taking Stella to the doctor for checkups and keeping Marion off the bottle. But the fact that he is still with a family makes it worth while and he is both happy and somewhat wistfully jealous that Alan was going to be a father. He wishes he had a child, "something substantial, something definite to look forward to: a male child, a projection of yourself into a future you would not otherwise know" (188). During Alan's absence, and he is away quite a bit, Ian and Stella draw close together although nothing serious develops between them. Ian cures Marion of her dependence on the bottle, sees the birth of Alan's male child, then leaves Aylward to go to Wendover.

A Male Child is a psychological gothic novel with the kind of Brontean and Jamesian atmosphere found in *Wuthering Heights* and *Turn of the Screw*. The characters in *A Male Child* are carefully analyzed, and Scott reveals himself as an anatomist of human emotions which he probes and dissects, layer by layer. In laying bare the family secrets at Aylward, Ian lays himself out for dissection. It is a well crafted novel, divided into three sections: seed, gestation, and parturition. Ian Canning's personal story holds our attention, and the novel which begins with his wife's abortion, concludes with the life proclaiming cry of Alan's male child. In Ian's inability to find and hold on to a job, partly because of his illness, and hence unable to lead a full life, Scott once again emphasizes his theme of the importance of work in the lives of the men he writes about. Scott has an ear for dialogue and a knack for setting a scene to bring out subtleties of conflict and character.

Both in the grace and felicity of style and sureness of plot and character, *A Male Child* reveals remarkable progress from the somewhat stilted and wooden style of *Johnnie Sahib*.

II The Bender

Paul Scott aptly described *The Bender* as a "sad comedy," a description that he was to apply to his last novel *Staying On*, which he termed "an Indian Bender."[2]

George Lisle-Spruce (note the hyphen, George's own word),

nicknamed Silky because of the Lisle, is divorced from his wife Alice, whom he had met and married in Cairo. He is childless, a secret between himself and Dr. Honeydew, because he is sterile from a case of mumps he had during his puberty. He is jobless. Even the jobs he has had thus far cannot be called real jobs: "helping somebody who knew somebody to sell something somebody else had got and somebody else wanted" (190). He has lived by his wits and charms thus far, but is now facing a crisis. *The Bender* is forty-eight hours in the life of George as he resolves this crisis.

When George was a young man he had been left a legacy of ten thousand pounds by a distant relative, Sir Roderick Butterfield. Under the terms of this will, George would get only the annual income from this investment, about four hundred pounds a year— while the main amount was held in trust for his eldest child or his brother Tim's eldest child, should George die childless. Unfortunately, the "legacy was not enough to live on in any sort of style but it had begun by being too much in the absence of any other incentive to provide an incentive to work, and rot had not so much set in as bloomed creatively like a flower" (17).

In one of his innumerable odd jobs, in a drinking club, George had embezzled funds. "Borrowed it without their knowledge" (82) is the way he describes it, and he was saved from disgrace and jail by a loan of two hundred pounds from his brother Tim. Now, after years of patient waiting, Tim, a prosperous accountant on the rise in the firm of Bartle Wallingford and Co., wants repayment of that loan. Tim himself is facing a personal crisis. His seventeen-year-old daughter Gillian who calls herself "basically existentialist" (82) is pregnant with the child of Click Clayton, a plumber's mate. Tim needs money to meet the extra expenses involved in taking care of his daughter's problem.

George is not too keen on helping his brother Tim, but he likes his niece Gillian for whom he is godfather. To get out of this mess, George sees four courses of action, all unpleasant. He can handle two odd jobs: become a teddy bear salesman or become chauffeur for a man called Mick, who runs a call girl service. The third alternative would be to ask Aunt Clara who might refuse, which would leave him with the fourth and last course: commit suicide. This would not give Tim back his loan but would give Gillian a fortune.

Unable to decide, George does the only thing he knows how to do. He goes on a bender, on a drinking marathon in pub after pub. Liquor loosens his tongue, and he talks to anyone who would listen, and when his audience runs out, George soliloquizes. It is in these outpourings, however, that George begins to see the truth about himself and realizes that he has been played a foul trick by that legacy. On the surface it had made George a man of means, but in reality had robbed him of motivation, of the need to find and hold on to a job he would be proud of. The legacy had left him adrift. George realizes that he is not properly defined, that he is half a man because he has no proper profession. He remembers Stendhal's *Souvenirs d' Egotisme* that he had been reading in translation, and remembers the statement, *Without work the vessel of life has no ballast* (17). Thus in George and his self-examination, Scott expresses his theme of man in relation to his work.

George's bender illuminates him but also ends in his passing out slumped on a sidestreet. He is picked up by the police and worms himself out of their clutches and ends up in his brother Tim's house. Tim attempts to buy off George. He offers to forget the loan and, in addition, promises fifty pounds if George would agree not to see Gillian until she has had her child and had it adopted by some interested couple.

A loan wiped out and fifty pounds in his pocket—the offer is tempting. But George, who has been reflecting on his wasted life thus far, refuses to be bought so easily. After all, Gillian is his goddaughter, his heir, because he is sterile. He decides not to let her down.

George's stand pays off, for he is asked by Tim's wife if he would accept a job, the job of looking after Gillian in the country while she awaits the birth of her child. For this service, the loan will be written off. George accepts because he knows that once Gillian sees the baby, she would think twice before putting up the baby for adoption. Maybe never, for the baby is after all George's heir. It gives him a sense of purpose, and he is so delighted that he even calls up his divorced wife to give her the good news.

The Bender deals with money or the lack of it. The minutiae of money, the mysteries of accounting, is rare in fiction. Seldom has a novelist gone into the details of everyday expense involved in the matter of living as Scott does in *The Bender*.

It is the inability of George to pay back his loan of two hundred pounds to his brother Tim that sets the stage for *The Bender*. It is George's inheritance of four hundred pounds per annum that has acted as an albatross around his neck, taking away the "hunger" for a job.

George is forever taking stock of his assets and liabilities, mentally counting his money, "change from his last pound note, ten and two pence, plus ten shillings and six pence in pennies and six pences, less three pence for the Evening Standard" (64). He is acutely aware of his dwindling pennies because, "there was simply no telling what challenges his money would have to face up to and tackle, but better by far the spent bob than the saved half-crown, because the spent bob was positive while the saved half-crown was negative. The one had life-force and the other didn't" (64).

At the other end of George's scramble for pennies is the prosperous gilt-edged world represented by the accounting firm of Bartle Wallingford and Co. The conversation, discussion, and transaction here is all in stocks and shares, partnerships and dividends, old money and new money, carried on in plush, carpeted rooms and sumptuous lunches at Simpsons. Scott draws upon his knowledge of accounting and money from his early career as an accountant as he describes these contrasting worlds of money and finance.

The Bender, in the words of Anthony Burgess, is "a superb comic novel based on contemporary England."[3] The sights and sounds of London life are presented effectively in passages of beauty and lucidity, whether it is at nighttime when the city is abandoned or inside a pub; whether in a park or inside a fast food place. Casual references to India are of course scattered throughout the novel.

The Bender reveals Scott's ear for dialogue and for recording the subtle nuances in conversation. There are two episodes in *The Bender* that could easily be turned into a two-act play. They come one after another in chapters 25 and 26.

There is old Wallingford representing the "cult of privilege" being eased out by the "cult of brains" represented by Tim Spruce. Tim Spruce, who would not have said "boo to a goose twenty five years ago" (115), is now telling sixty-five-year-old Wallingford, who had all the proper solid background, school, club, marriage, what he has got to do! The dialogue between Spruce and Wallingford is dramatic and scintillating. Following this chapter we have a highly animated, gossipy, sparkling conversation between the two secretaries of the firm, Millicent Maple and Connie Crayfoot. They have heard the rumors of Wallingford, "a gentleman born" although "a bit of an old woman" (122), leaving the firm and Spruce, with his craze for making records of every telephone conversation, taking over. In between their giggles and bites into a Wimpy, they discuss what took place. It is a hilarious piece of writing and Scott captures perfectly their accents and gossipy chatter, emphasised by their inimitable gestures as he portrays the world of the office secretaries, on their lunch breaks.

, The two chapters successively following each other present two versions of the same story, a narrative technique Scott was to use most effectively in *The Raj Quartet*.

The Bender, above all, reveals Scott's abilities for writing comedy with an undertone of sadness, a talent which he reveals again in his last novel, *Staying On*.

CHAPTER 4

The Corrida at San Feliu:
The Writer's Notebook as Novel

F ROM 1958 through 1963 Scott made an annual summer visit to Spain. From these visits he fashioned *The Corrida at San Feliu*, the setting of which is both India and Spain, territories familiar to Scott.

The Corrida is a novel about a novelist writing a novel, rather facing more than the usual creative problems with it. In writing about a writer, to whom writing is life and the inability to write is impotence and death, Scott continues his metaphor of man in relationship to his work. It is a complex but fascinating work which illuminates the craft of writing fiction. It defies easy summary because the chronology is topsy-turvy; the same characters take on different names; events are shifted to different locales as illusion competes with reality, and Scott explores the creative process as it applies to novelists, specifically, the exploration of the relationship between a novelist and his material.

The novelist is Edward Thornhill, "a genuine tragic figure," according to Anthony Burgess.[1] Thornhill is an American, sixty years old and aging, suffering from the lingering and possibly terminal illness of the burned out writer. Since the publication four years ago of his last novel, *Cassandra Laughing*, a novel about human optimism, Thornhill's new novel has been stuck in the typewriter.

Thornhill and his wife Myra, twenty years younger than him, had been living in a villa in a small resort on the Costa Brava in Spain. On a return trip from Barcelona, where they had gone to meet Thornhill's publisher, they meet with a fatal automobile accident, perhaps willfully contrived by Thornhill. His publisher gathers together Thornhill's manuscripts and notebooks, has a preface written to introduce him, and *The Corrida* is published.

The Corrida is made up of two parts. Part 1 is titled *Preface and Papers*. In the chapter titled "Edward Thornhill: A Preface," Scott invents the hypothetical novelist Edward Thornhill, based "not only upon the notes that Thornhill left behind . . . but also upon knowledge gained of Thornhill through a long personal and business association" (10). But the preface is more than the factual biography of Thornhill. It is a careful and clear statement of Thornhill's views on the art of writing the novel, which are those of Paul Scott himself, as we will see later in this chapter.

Part 1 is also made up of Thornhill's preliminary stories, such as "The Leopard Mountain," completed or scarcely begun, and three attempts at the novel he was writing: "The First Betrayal," "The Arrival in Playa de Faro," and "The Arrival in Mahwar."

"The Leopard Mountain," an allegorical short story, is set in Africa and concerns human greed and stupidity. It is the tale of a wealthy scrap merchant, a whiteman in Africa, "who couldn't bear the thought of anything belonging to anyone else" (20), who is upset when he hears from an African native boy that a female leopard thought of the area around the mountain as her own and lorded it over the surrounding wilderness. Saunders decides to kill the leopard and "hang its skin on the walls of his living-room as proof of the futility of possessiveness in all dumb creatures" (20).

It is an excellent story, "as fine a piece of writing as anything done on Africa by Hemingway."[2] Although Scott has said that he always needed a broad canvas to write, and hence had never written a short story,[3] "The Leopard Mountain" seems to be an exception to that statement. It is a story that lends itself perfectly for anthologizing in a volume of short stories.

Part 2 consists of the much longer "Plaza de Toros." Autobiographical and "intensely personal" (9), it is a "personal investigation into his obsession with the incapacity of men and women to love unselfishly, with its curious and colorful imagery, that of the Corrida, the last pagan spectacle in the civilised world" (9).

The Corrida is therefore presented as a posthumous publication of the fictional novelist Edward Thornhill.

The theme of the novel Thornhill was writing at the time of his death "was about two people who turned up somewhere in disgrace" (8). In his first attempt at this novel he has them showing up in India, at a Dak Bungalow, in the chapter titled, "The First Betrayal." They are nameless at this stage, the man, "with a long thin melancholy face" (53), later given the name of Bruce, and the woman, later called

Thelma, has her face "shaded by a wide-brimmed solar topee" (53). They are "cut dead" by Major and Mrs. Clipsby-Smith, prominent members of the tight knit, socially caste conscious, British colonial community. Such an introduction to these two people, Bruce and Thelma, Thornhill had hoped would make the reader wonder what the man and woman had done. "I suppose," Thornhill answers his own question, "they've committed some awful breach of rules and regulations. I mean people have sent them to coventry, and they've come all this way to Darshansingh to hide their faces. I wonder where they're staying. Probably some bungalow in the jungle, between here and Mahwar, full of ghosts" (55).

The image and the aura of mystery pleases Thornhill. But he abandons it.

So he makes another attempt, a fresh start, in "The Arrival in Playa de Faro," to introduce the two people turning up in disgrace. This time they arrive with names—Bruce and Thelma—and with luggage "encrusted with travel labels as if it belonged to a party of vagabond harlequins" (67). The place is now the ritzy jet-set vacation spot, the playa de faro. Bruce and Thelma are the beautiful people. She is thirty-nine and he is fifty. He is "mahogany naked from the waist up" (67), and is proudly displaying his healthy bronzed body dressed in "washed out blue jeans which cleave his buttocks" (67). She has "a gold charm bracelet jingling on her wrist" (67), and her hair has the color of "gold-in-the-iron sculptural quality you associate with the word bronze" (67), but when she bends her head to be dried in the sun "you could see how pale and yellow it was at the roots in the nape of her neck" (67).

No, this is not right either. So Thornhill "tried it another way" (52). Thornhill shifts his two people turning up in disgrace back in India. In "The Arrival in Mahwar," Bruce and Thelma Craddock arrive in Mahwar at the Panther House, a place once described by an Englishman who had lived there as "this murderous spot" (71).

In this third attempt, Bruce and Thelma are at the end of their ropes—Thelma, in particular, with her "brown lustreless" hair clinging to her scalp, "laughing hysterically" while Bruce "jerks her rag doll body" (70) and strikes her on the cheeks.

In this attempt, Thornhill reveals the reason for Bruce and Thelma showing up in disgrace. Infidelity on the part of Thelma who had been christened Lesley as a child, and had fallen for Bruce, a married man, and suicide by her husband Ned Pearson, who had been unable to face up to the harsh reality of his wife falling for a younger man of a junior rank in his own company. Ned Pearson had shot himself because of the disgrace, and Bruce and Thelma had moved from place to place, showing up in disgrace wherever they went.

At this stage, Thornhill's novel-in-progress with its various attempts at fresh new starts had gotten stuck.

It is in part 2, "The Plaza de Toros," the autobiographical section, that we find out why Thornhill had not been able to make significant progress with his novel about two people turning up in disgrace. What Thornhill was attempting to write was intensely personal, so personal that he did not want to face the truth about it. But in abandoning the form of the novel and turning to autobiography, Thornhill discovers in the blinding light of intense self-analysis the truth about himself. "The truth did not come to me suddenly. It came quietly, circumspectly, sniffling and whimpering, looking to be let in many times before" (156). Truth forces Thornhill out into the open, like the bull which ultimately has to come out of the "cuernica"—that place of refuge—for the dangerous sun-bright arena. These constant changes in his attempted novel, "plays within plays such as made a King and Queen squirm in their chairs one night in the rotten state of Denmark" (202), makes Thornhill face up to the truth that the two people who turned up in disgrace were none other than he and his young wife Myra. "It was I and Myra who had turned up in disgrace. The Craddocks were pictures I had drawn on a mirror so that I should not have to face the truth directly" (156). Thus in wanting to write about two people, Thornhill has been trying to write about himself. Thornhill is old; his wife, Myra, is still young and desirable. She is the only thing he has left. Of course he has his writing, but that can be no substitute for love. Thornhill is consumed by jealousy, for his wife Myra has an affair with the handsome youth he refers to as godling, a young Poseidon "emerging from the sea . . . [in] his blue satin bulge" (110). This jealousy consumes Thornhill and cripples him. It also fills him with a martyrdom kind of self-pity as his feverish imagination conjures up these illicit meetings between his wife and the godling.

The jealousy which consumes him has been a pleasant agony. He has luxuriated in it, enjoyed it. Jealousy has made Thornhill into a peeping tom, turned him into an obsessive voyeur upon his own life, and obstructed his creative faculties. His beautiful wife and his unfinished novel are both unfaithful to him. It has made him lose the sense of control so essential to a novelist. Thornhill has never subscribed to the character-take-over theory of the novel: "They don't run away with you. You have to lead them carefully step by step to their logical conclusion, and you have to stop leading them if the conclusion doesn't fit in with the original picture of them" (78).

In the novel, Thornhill had attempted to write about two people showing up in disgrace: instead of controlling his two characters, he has allowed himself to be controlled by them. Myra and the godling, with their clandestine trysting places, and their "curious rituals of their morning assignation" (174), have hypnotized Thornhill. He has become passive. The bull leads the bullfighter instead of the bullfighter challenging the bull and being in command of the situation.

Now that Thornhill realizes what has gone wrong with his novel-in-progress, he decides to bring it into focus. In the novel he was writing, the character of Ned Pearson is Thornhill's alter ego. Ned Pearson too has been cuckolded and is unable to bear the shame and humiliation brought on by the infidelity of his wife. So Ned sets up his "monkish, military room that was his office as if for a court martial" (72), strips himself of his buttons and insignia of rank, and standing against a wall shoots himself through the head.

Looking back on this "ending," rereading this part of his novel-in-progress, Thornhill knows what he must do. But he still lacks the "courage or is it the conviction?" of what he must do, to successfully and aesthetically fuse experience and art. "After a lifetime spent in observing and commenting on human behaviour he seems to find it difficult to understand his own" (174).

Thornhill sets himself up to look at himself "objectively, on what turns out to be the last day of his life" (173). And here is Thornhill's own picture of himself, "the face of a man ruined by his own curiosity" (82). "A tall man of sixty clothed en fete in blue terylene trousers and crimson shantung silk shirt, with bare feet tucked into canvas espadrilles" (172).

He takes himself to the corrida in San Feliu, to watch the pagan spectacle of the bullfight in the corrida, and observe the "three fights going on at any time in the plaza when a corrida is in progress: The fight the bull puts up, the fight the torero tries to conduct, and the fight the spectators think they see" (201).

Thornhill sits watching the corrida, "waiting for the personal revelation of what he really means when he says, as he has said so often, so glibly, for nearly sixty years: I love, I care, let justice be done, teach us to forgive; hoping that . . . there will be a glimpse of the reality behind the illusion that a man can care for someone other than himself" (213). Thornhill sees it his duty to uncover and exorcise all such illusions. He has thus far lived under such an illusion. In that novel-in-progress, his alter ego, Ned Pearson, had shot himself, and now Thornhill plans and directs the death of both himself and his wife Myra. The ending of these lives becomes the ending of the novel as well.

The Corrida is a dazzling virtuoso performance. It was Paul Scott's favorite novel: "I thought it was a swan, but the critics thought it was a goose."[4]

The critics were indeed perplexed by *The Corrida*. Orville Prescott saw heavy-handed symbolism in it, and declared that nothing "was blindingly clear."[5] Of course, things are not blindingly clear; if they were, *The Corrida* would not have existed. It is because "things" are not blindingly clear to Thornhill that he faces his dilemma, his doubts and anxieties. *The Corrida* is the writer's notebook as novel, and it is only upon several readings that things do become clear, as it does to Thornhill himself.

Ernest Buckler, Canadian novelist and critic, thought that in *The Corrida* Paul Scott had made a valiant bid to outdo himself, and that it was both good and bad. He praised the technique of an Italian movie with its flashbacks and disjointed images, that Paul Scott has used to help build the novel to an unified effect, but stated that "cut by a third, the book would have been three times as good."[6]

M. W. Rodman saw in the craft of Paul Scott, the occupational hazard of the bullfighter, good with one bull, bad with another, and concluded that *The Corrida* was exciting as long as Scott was away from the bullring.[7]

Scott claims no expertise about tauromachy, acknowledging as he does that he owes his limited knowledge of the bullring to a number of books on bullfighting, in particular to Barnaby Conrad's *Encyclopaedia of Bullfighting*.[8] *The Corrida* has very little to do with tauromachy as such, for it is only used to symbolize the problem of the novelist Edward Thornhill. Speaking in the character of Thornhill, Scott dismisses the whole mystique of bullfighting as not his realm but that of Hemingway: "I had always kept away from Spain. For me it was the graveyard of the thirties and the literary preserve anyway of poor old Ernest" (78).

Robert Taubman called the novel obscure and insufficient, and saw in the novel's protagonist Edward Thornhill's inability to write a novel, the problem of Scott himself in stating the theme of the novel "unsuccessfully in different ways."[9]

Benny Green admirably highlights the importance of *The Corrida* among the novels of Scott. In writing *The Corrida*, Green says, "Scott tried to show us what can never effectively be shown, that is the relationship between a novelist and his material, and how that material is ingested by the creative process." He continues by noting that the interplay of biography and fictional writing may well be too subtle for the ordinary reader to bother much about, "but anyone who has ever attempted fiction, will find *The Corrida at San Feliu* an absorbing and educational experience."[10]

The prose of *The Corrida*, according to Maia Rodman, is lucid and clear and has "the grace of a torero wielding the muleta."[11] Passages describing the spectacle in the corrida have a music and rhythm that is uniquely Scott's.

The Corrida also contains a common stylistic device: "Regard him then," as Scott introduces a character, or "Imagine if you will," as he evokes a place or scene—phrases he was to use (as effectively as the baton in the maestro's hand) in *The Raj Quartet*, which begins with the evocative phrase: "Imagine, then, a flat landscape."

The Corrida also makes use of Scott's unique technique of seeing persons and events from different points of view, a technique that he was to perfect in telling the story of *The Raj Quartet*. We see Thornhill as his publisher saw him, and Thornhill as his wife saw him, Thornhill as seen by his wife's lover, and Thornhill as seen by himself "objectively." We see him, therefore, fictionally, biographically, and autobiographically. The result is a complex portrait of the total man, with that element of sphinxlike mystery which is at the heart of all great fiction.

The novel is strewn with apt descriptions of people and places. Mrs. Clipsby-Smith, the British woman, "an unlikely sparrow of a woman" who appears briefly in one of the begun but abandoned attempts by Thornhill, is thus evoked: "[She] was a bead twister. She had a stringy neck, no bosom, and a habit of never keeping her head still . . . her eyes were staring into those vague mists that swirl about the private twilight world of unaccountable failure and distant deprivation" (49).

Then there is the picture of the Eurasian, half-caste girl, Leela, who makes a brief appearance in the section of Thornhill's novel placed in India. "She had her mother's, not her father's bones. The creamy, only slightly tinted flesh was stretched fine, almost transparently over them . . . like so many Indian women she was built for burning. Dry and brittle in the body, she would be gone in the first lick of flame, all except her eyes, through which so far she had seen nothing of the world; through which . . . she conveyed something of her great untapped capacity for living" (147).

And then the very apt description of Myra, Thornhill's wife: "She had the kind of looks that made her welcome everywhere and feel welcome nowhere" (93).

There is something of Scott in Thornhill. Like Scott, Thornhill is anticolonialist, and like Scott who was later to author *The Raj Quartet,* the elegy for the decline of the British Empire, Thornhill too has written a trio of novels in sequence dealing with colonial life: *The District Commissioner; The House of Cards;* and *The Administrators.* Thornhill calls his British the lost administrators, "a dead race now; as dead as the last Romans in a no longer savage Britain" (109).

But it is in his definitive views and perspectives on writing that Thornhill often becomes the spokesman for his creator Scott. Take the important need for control within a novel. When Thornhill says that characters do not run away, that they have to be directed step by step, he is echoing Scott's own belief. In an interview Scott had stated, "A novelist must be in control within the novel. It is the author who controls, not the character. I have no belief in the character took over concept."[12]

Speaking of words and their usage, that essential tool of the writer, Thornhill refers to words having meaning as an onion has skins, and admires the Spaniards who "pronounce every letter of their angular language. They know words come hard and don't waste them by throwing parts of them away" (90). Scott too believed in the wisdom of using words carefully, sparingly. He called it part of his puritanism. "Words are my business and I use them carefully. It is probably because of this, that I have never maintained notebooks or journals, for by using words unnecessarily, I do no want them to lose their strength."[13]

It is however with Thornhill's credo, about the writer and his craft, that he can be looked upon as Scott's alter ego.

The work is all that matters. It stands or falls by itself. But it stands or falls as a game. As a writer I do not feel that I have any special duty to society or feel, as a writer, that I should have any expectations or desire or hope of improving it or making it wiser or more tolerant, either by example, entreaty, satire, castigation, cheers or catcalls. I do not see myself, as a novelist, as a man whose opinions on the burning questions of the day are of any outstanding importance. As a man in society I vote, pay taxes, have opinions and argue with my neighbour when sober enough to understand what I am asked to support or drunk enough to find colorful words to refute. But as a man who writes what is called fiction I play no tune and dance to none, for in that capacity I am concerned not with panaceas, but with questions unsusceptible even of formulation. (18)

Scott, too, as Benny Green points out, "sought no publicity, joined no schools, expressed no opinions but simply did the only real literary work, which is to get on with the task of discovering your own uniqueness."[14]

In *The Corrida*, Scott deals with the complex and important theme of the evolution of a writer's craft and the use of fictional imagination in transforming personal experiences into art. It is a richly textured novel, and autobiographical in terms of expressing Scott's perspectives on the art of writing. Because of these qualities, *The Corrida* is Scott's most significant novel after *The Raj Quartet*.

CHAPTER 5

Pointing to The Raj Quartet

S COTT'S second novel, *The Alien Sky* (1953), his fourth, *The Mark of the Warrior* (1958), his fifth and sixth, *The Chinese Love Pavilion* (1960) and *The Birds of Paradise* (1962) respectively, have one thing in common: they all reveal in varying degrees of story, style, and theme, Scott "warming up" for *The Raj Quartet*.

Of this group of four novels, *The Alien Sky* and *The Birds of Paradise* are much closer to *The Raj Quartet* than *The Mark of the Warrior* and *The Chinese Love Pavilion*. But the latter novels do contain certain themes that were to find larger and fuller treatment in *The Raj Quartet*.

All four of them—Tom Gower in *The Alien Sky*; Tom Brent in *The Chinese Love Pavilion*: Conway, Daintree, and Cranston in *The Birds of Paradise*; and Craig in *The Mark of the Warrior*—continue to interpret Scott's metaphor of men in relationship to their jobs.

While *The Mark of the Warrior* and *The Birds of Paradise* reveal Scott's consummate skills both as novelist and craftsman, *The Alien Sky* and *The Chinese Love Pavilion* reflect his weaknesses and represent the two low points in his writing career.

I The Alien Sky

India, June, 1947, two months before the announced departure of the British from the subcontinent is the place and time of *The Alien Sky*.

The novel concerns itself with an assorted group of Britishers and Indians, their interaction with each other, and their varied responses to the withdrawal of the British Raj. In particular, *The Alien Sky* is about Tom Gower, "an Englishman to whom Indian independence meant losing a job he loved,"[1] and facing the prospect of being uprooted.

The place is Marapore (not to be confused with Mayapore, a locale which features prominently in the later novel sequence, *The Raj Quartet*), a small British residential area adjacent to the neighboring princely state of Kalipur. But with independence in the air for all of the subcontinent, and the imminent prospect of a political operation to bifurcate India into two nations—India and Pakistan—Kalipur's chances for survival as an independent entity are very slim. It is the future of Kalipur as well as the future of the British colonial community in Marapore that constitutes the heart of the novel.

To Marapore from Calcutta comes Joe McKendrick, an American Sahib accompanied by his Indian servant, Bholu. "Vacation" is the reason McKendrick gives for his visit to Marapore. But his real purpose is to find Dorothy Gower, whose picture and letter had been found in the wallet of his dead brother, Dwight.

Dorothy is the sullen wife of Tom Gower, an idealistic Englishman to whom India is home. Gower identifies himself with the Indians, and their cause for independence. He operates a model farm at Ooni, a few miles away from Marapore, and serves as editor of *The Marapore Gazette*, a position to which he has been appointed by Nayar, a wealthy Indian.

As the novel opens, Gower has written an editorial in which he has proposed that since Pakistan is a fait accompli, the idea and the new nation be accepted wholeheartedly. He has also naively suggested that the state of Kalipur retain its independence and not accede to either India or Pakistan. A brilliant but radical student, Vidyasagar turns the prize-giving ceremony for sports at the local college to a rally against Gower. Thus Tom Gower, beloved of the Indians, becomes overnight their archenemy. "Go home Gower" graffiti and banner signs proliferate. He loses his editorial position on the paper.

McKendrick is a spectator of these turbulent events marking "the last days of the British Raj" and is invited to attend a party given by an Englishman, Sanderson. Here he runs into an Indian journalist, Gupta, a former editor of *The Mayapore Gazette* and a member of the militant Hindu political party, the R.S.S. Gupta strongly condemns Tom Gower's editorial as an interference in Indian affairs. He cynically tells McKendrick that the party he is attending is a fraternisation party, held "in most cases in the out-of-doors. At one end of the lawn there will be gathered the representatives of the Raj, and at the other those of us who have passed some test of whose nature we are not aware but the reward for which is the invitation to the party" (43–44).

The only friend Tom Gower wins from his editorial is the Maharajah of Kalipur, popularly known by his pseudonym, Jimmy

Smith. Looking like "a bright eyed, mischievous, well fed bird," he struts around "on his short stocky legs" (56), trying to discover who this admirable Gower is. Sight unseen he offers Gower a job in an independent Kalipur, both still born and nonexistent. Gower is eager to accept the job. He cannot go back to England because there is nothing worthwhile in England for a man like him. He acutely feels his social outcast position, a feeling intensified by the lack of sympathy and support from his wife, Dorothy.

Dorothy too has her private problems. On the one hand, she wants her husband to lose his job, be encircled in hate, so that he would be forced to leave India. Yet, Dorothy is not quite ready to go to England. Like Tom, she will not be at home in England, a place she has always called "home." Dorothy, for all her outward appearance and carefully contrived background as the only daughter of a deceased British tea planter, is really the result of a one night stand affair between an English soldier and an Indian woman. Ashamed of her mixed blood, she has concealed it from Tom and the others. Her past limits her socially, and she dreads running into another Eurasian, Judith Anderson, who knows her secret. However, in a moment of complete trust, after a brief affair in Calcutta with Dwight, brother of Joe McKendrick, she had shared her secret with him. But he too gives her the cold shoulder. She strongly feels the burden of her racial mixture, and in her desire to maintain the lie she has created lets herself be victimized by a blackmailer.

Dorothy's silence and her bursts of ill temper lead Tom Gower to the conclusion that she is in love with someone else. Possibly his assistant at the model farm in Ooni, Joe Steele, another Englishman.

Joe Steele is a man of action first and thought later. He has no love for Dorothy, for he alone among the Mayapore British crowd knows that she is not English, and despises her for giving herself a heritage to which she is not entitled. Joe Steele has an Indian girl of his own, pregnant with his child.

There is a confrontation between Joe and Tom but it is overshadowed by other events such as a strike by the employees on the farm. The peaceful strike erupts into violence and Dass, a prominent Indian worker, is severely wounded. The entire Indian staff leaves the farm and violence spreads from Ooni to Mayapore. Militant political groups, both Hindu (R.S.S.) and Muslim (the Khaksars), flail the flames of passion and prejudice and in the confusion Bholu, Joe McKendrick's servant, is shot and killed by Joe Steele. Bholu turns out to have been the blackmailer of Dorothy.

Bholu's death becomes a symbol of British oppression and a

rallying cry for the radical groups. So an inquest is held. "Pure formality. The Indians love it. They've great respect for courts and such like," the district magistrate explains to Steele. Besides, he adds "there's no reason why we shouldn't give them another example of the incorruptibility of British Justice" (173). But on his way to the inquest, Vidyasagar, the student, the true fanatic, shoots and kills Joe Steele.

Tom Gower, now mistakenly again, believes that it is Joe McKendrick with whom his wife has been having an affair, and warns him to keep off. Joe McKendrick secretly communicates with Dorothy, offering to take her away with him. Dorothy secretly plans to leave with McKendrick and calls her husband "physically repulsive" (197).

Rejected by his wife; by Indians whom he had befriended; jobless because Jimmy Smith the Maharajah who had offered him a job is having problems of his own, Tom Gower attempts suicide. This act of Tom's shakes up Dorothy, who returns to Tom and to Marapore.

The Alien Sky is a rather glib, conventional Anglo-Indian novel. The various characters in the novel represent different political types or attitudes. There is the liberal do-gooder, Tom Gower; the political man of action, Joe Steele; the interfering, aggressive American, Joe McKendrick; the bumbling, spoiled caricature of a Maharajah, Jimmy Smith; the pathetic Eurasians, Dorothy Gower and Judith Anderson, loyal to an England which does not want them and an India that despises them; there is the strong imperialist English colonial represented in Cynthia Mapelton, a Memsahib for ten years who is planning on going to Kenya, for she has developed a taste for being waited on by colored servants; there is the forever India hand in Miss Harriett Haig, one time governess to the Maharajah of Kalipur, who will die in India because to her England is not home; there is the radical student Vidyasagar; and the conniving politicians Gupta and Nayar.

The careful layer by layer analysis, and self-introspection of character and motive that Scott reveals so admirably in his later novels, is conspicuously absent in *The Alien Sky*.

The story line is equally contrived, and the last parts of the novel, with its shoot-outs and quick changes of character, declines to sheer old-time Hollywood movie melodrama about British "Indjyah"!

The Alien Sky touches on themes that Scott was to develop with greater understanding and insight in his later works. The problems and dilemmas faced by the princely states when independence came, as in the case of Kalipur, is given excellent treatment in *The Birds of*

Paradise. And the theme of the impact of independence on those Englishmen who did not want to return to England, like Tom Gower, finds an impressive emotional and artistic expression in Scott's final novel *Staying On.* Even some of the characters such as the radical student Vidyasagar, is developed into a much more believable character when he appears in *The Jewel in the Crown*, the first volume of *The Raj Quartet.*

The Alien Sky is a very rough draft of a period and a place Scott was to explore in all his later novels. This is its only significance to a student of Scott's writings.

II   The Chinese Love Pavilion

The Chinese Love Pavilion (published in the United States as *The Love Pavilion*, a reflection of the political mood of the 1960s toward China) concerns itself with "Madness brought on by obsession with occupations for their own sakes—occupations disrupted or invented by war."[2]

The novel introduces us at the very beginning to the Love Pavilion and its one time inhabitant Teenachang. The Pavilion, amid the forest and hills of Bukit-Kallang, in Malaya, built by a Chinese merchant who had made his fortune in Malaya and later executed by the Japanese invaders, was aggressively Oriental and contained four rooms. It was in the room with no name, the anteroom, that Teenachang, "the most beautiful woman in Malaya" (9), lived when Tom Brent, the narrator of the novel, met her. "Teena was half Chinese, one-quarter Dutch, one-quarter French, Christian by upbringing, a prostitute by profession" (9), and presided over the Love Pavilion surrounded by her wealth; "baubles mostly, silks from Hong Kong, jewelery from Bangkok, silk stockings from New York, hand bags from Rome, shoes from Paris, a shawl from Kashmir, and creams and powders from Hollywood" (12)—and a kris, the traditional Malayan dagger, the handle set with semiprecious stones and impeccable workmanship, given by Tom Brent.

The story of *The Pavilion* is the story of Tom Brent and begins before the war in India. Tom Brent, whose ancestors had a tradition of service in India, had long dreamed of a military career in India. But, at the age of sixteen, he abandoned Kipling for Forster and decided on a civil service career, that of a benign and wise district commissioner. Even this he later abandons, because he does not want to be a part of British imperialism.

Bound to India as he was emotionally, he departs for Bombay at the age of twenty-one, not as a Sahib but as a common worker, "to live on the lowest level of Sub-European Society" (16) doing clerical work—"Under and not over an Indian" (19). He lives in a hotel run by a Mrs. Ross, a dark-skinned Eurasian woman, insisting he be called "Tom" and not Mr. Brent. This romantic democratic approach lasts two months, at the end of which Tom realizes that his escapade was a failure, the Indian inheritance an illusion, and decides to return to England.

At this juncture enters Brian Saxby, at Mrs. Ross's hostelry like someone from "a story by Conan Doyle" (21). Saxby, who had come out East at the age of twenty in search of plants and people, mesmerizes Tom with his talk. He quotes Conrad, that when a man is born he is flung into a dream as if into a sea and that man must pursue that dream if he wants a purpose. He calls Tom "a coal heaver," Saxby's description for a romantic who wants to work with his hands, and counsels Tom to fall into his dream and give it a purpose. He wants Tom to go with him to meet a man called Greystone.

Tom heads North with Saxby to Rajputana and the Punjab on "a voyage of discovery and rediscovery" (38). It is a fascinating journey across a "land's land, too vast, too beautiful to harbour well the designs men sought to carve upon it" (39). They turn south and enter Greystone's valley to meet the "man who had fought authority most of his life" (40). Greystone has a mystical conception of the land and is involved in rehabilitating a dry and barren land. Saxby leaves, but Tom stays and works for Greystone on the stubborn land for four years.

Tom had found his vocation through Saxby, and Greystone had shown him how to follow it through. But, "the monotony of one man's companionship stretching out into the future threatened to become intolerable" (44), and Tom grows restless.

A visit from Saxby, who accuses Tom that he now has both the face and mind of a Sahib and that he has merely accepted Greystone's authority, makes Tom take a hard look at himself. Saxby invites him to go with him to Malaya to collect plants. The idea of a trip to Malaya catches fire, and Tom sets out.

Saxby is in Singaputan, a remote spot in the Malayan Jungle. Amid his trays of potted plants, which hang, climb, convolute all around him, Saxby sits on a wicker chair "diminished almost beyond recognition" (57). He greets Tom, provides him with food, drink, and even an untouchable virgin girl for his companionship.

Saxby has changed. "My body has its functions but no enchantments" (62), he declares and talks disparagingly about what had once been his passion, the collection and study of plants. It is now so much waste to him. "Waste—myself—committed to the collection of other waste, plants. I collect plants, but I don't *explore* them" (62). Saxby can no longer give Tom renewed belief in his spiritual existence.

Frustrated and angry, because Saxby had wasted his time, spoiled his holiday, and "cast a shadow on all the better times" (69) they had had together, Tom leaves for Singapore. In Singapore Tom buys the jewelled kris which he six years later gives to Teenachang, the presiding mistress of the Love Pavilion.

The six-year period is covered briefly in the novel: Tom is wounded in the war, permanently disfigured and handicapped by a shell splinter carving out a piece of his right shoulder; Greystone dies; Saxby's whereabouts are not known.

Then comes the war and Tom, a major in the army, is summoned by Major Turner to whom "Saxby's been an obsession . . . for three years" (43). This not only stirs up Tom's memories of the man but starts him on a search for him.

From Major Turner, Tom learns that Saxby had "become committed to something" (75) again; that Saxby had teamed up with a band of Malayan guerillas fighting the Japanese, smoking them out of their jungle hideouts; that Saxby had lived for some time with the Sakai, aborigines of the Malayan interior, but that now he was "a bloody hulk of a man with a flaming red beard who seemed to think he was God and made you feel like dirt" (75). The disturbing fact was that Saxby had planned ruthless raids on the Japanese, captured and gagged them and burned them alive soaked in petrol (76). Saxby had produced a vision all his own, for something to believe in, so that he could go around on his self-appointed mission to carry out his private vendetta, using his hallmark, fire. All this had, of course, turned Saxby into a legend. The Japanese had put a price on his head. Turner wants Tom to find Saxby because he alone can recognize Saxby. Tom remembers the tag that Saxby used to wear, "This animal is in need of care and attention" (85) and reflecting that "one man, wandering from his tribe, diminishes" (85) all of mankind, accepts the assignment. He heads to Bukit-Kallang to begin his hunt for Saxby.

It is on his search for Saxby that Tom comes across the Love Pavilion and is initiated into its mysteries.

Major Reid, commandant in charge of Bukit-Kallang, his second-in-command Calthorp, and MacAndrews, another officer, all think that Saxby's dead. Over dinner they tell Tom that he's wasting his time looking for Saxby. But Tom Brent stays.

After dinner, Tom is taken to the Love Pavilion and introduced to Madame Chang (Teena). She becomes his girl for the night. In Teena Chang, Tom sees the face of the collaborator "invisible to the actual eye and only just to that of the mind" (113), and the thought of Saxby coming at him there and announcing himself in letters of fire makes him shudder.

Tom Brent meets some guerillas in Bukit-Kallang, among them Wan Lo who had worked with Saxby. Saxby was a very religious man, Wan Lo says, and often went in disguise like a Sikh staining his skin, dying his beard, and wearing a turban, accompanied by Al Choong, a Chinese boy.

Tom revisits Teena Chang to ask her if Saxby had come to see her. Yes, he had, to ask her to murder the Japanese officers when they came to visit her, and make a list of all collaborators. She had of course done neither. "When people say I collaborated all they're saying is I slept with them" (138), she tells Tom.

Tom's desire to hunt down Saxby turns into an obsession. He "could still smell Saxby. He was everywhere in the jungle" (16). And mysteriously, unexpectedly, one night while returning from Teena Chang's, Tom comes face to face with Saxby dressed like a Sikh. Tom recognizes him, and startles Saxby by calling him Brian, but the next second Tom is hit from behind and faints. The blow angers Tom, who now wants to go after Saxby to teach him that he could not get away after making an attempt to kill him.

Tom will not admit to Major Reid that he had seen Saxby. Major Reid, however, is convinced that Saxby is in the area and mounts a manhunt, operation S, but the S in operation S does not stand for Saxby; it stands for Sutton, a nineteen-year-old boy, a new recruit in Reid's outfit. Reid wants to use the Saxby manhunt for Sutton's initiation ceremony into masculinity.

Tom's search leads him to a cave, inside which is Saxby's satchel and in it his journal written in English. It is a record of Saxby's thoughts and feelings tracing his journey from a believer to a nonbeliever and his disgust at the torture meted out by the Japanese toward those they had conquered. He concludes by talking about his fight with his follower Ah Choong and being mortally wounded in the struggle and rapidly losing blood.

Tom wants desperately to find Saxby, and save him from his bleeding. But he is late. Saxby is found dead and lying on his bed of flowers.

Now that Saxby's business is over, Major Reid arranges for a bit of a show in the Love Pavilion: girls, Chinese crackers, and flamboyant dressing gowns. Unfortunately, Sutton goes berserk and kills Teena with the kris that Tom had given her as a gift. Sutton had killed her because he had been incapable of proving his manhood with her.

In looking back upon his nights of love with Teena in the Love Pavilion, Tom realizes that he had fallen in love with her; as for the scenes in the Pavilion which she had staged, she probably saw them "as symbols of the parodies of love" (253). And as for Saxby, the man who had filled him with an obsession, Tom prefers Saxby's brand of doubt to his own brand of faith.

The Pavilion is an uneven novel. The first part of the novel— concerned with Tom Brent's arrival in India, his meeting with Saxby, his work with Greystone, and rejoining Saxby briefly in Malaya—are all evoked with clarity and beauty. They constitute chapters in the education of a young man in an alien culture and are written with understanding and sensitivity. There is an element of elusive mystery in the portrait of Saxby that is natural, and he emerges larger than life. Tom's fascination with this man bordering on hero worship is equally realistic, and the relationship between them is the main strength of the first part.

The second part starts off well in linking Tom with Saxby after a six-year absence. Tom's search for the elusive Saxby has all the elements for a first-rate adventure story. Unfortunately, the story gets bogged down when Scott creates Saxby's philosophy of five souls, and attempts to integrate the rules of Sikhism with it. The carefully conceived character of Saxby disintegrates under the weight of heavy and even pretentious symbolism.

The concluding third part of the novel, where Saxby is finally discovered dead and Teena Chang is killed by Sutton, is anti-climactic. It is cluttered with too much symbolism to give the entire novel a coherent tightly knit structure.

Was it the education and coming into manhood of an Englishman that Scott was attempting? Was it a sheer good adventure story he was trying to tell? Was it the pursuit of a hero and his dream by a young, starry-eyed romantic boy? Or was it a combination of all these against the exotic backgrounds of India and Malaya?

If Scott had answered these questions clearly, *The Love Pavilion* could have developed a focal point, and the two weak parts of the novel could have been orchestrated with proper rhythm to match the narrative power and craftsmanship of the first part of the novel.

Thus, in attempting to blend the "suspenseful romantic-touch erotic-nostalgic adventure with Conradian mystical defeatism,"[3] Scott failed to come to grips with his material.

The control of story and character within a novel, qualities so highly valued by Scott, is missing in *The Pavilion*. Both Saxby and the story have run away from the author and got entangled and lost in the wild jungles of images and symbols.

III   The Mark of the Warrior

The Mark of the Warrior, is "about an officer in India obsessed with the idea that men had died because he had not done his job properly and that his job now was to bring out in a young cadet those qualities he lacked himself which he thought important."[4]

In the Burmese Campaign of May, 1942, Major Colin Craig was commanding officer of an Indian rifle company. They were in retreat from the Japanese and "moving in a North-Western direction toward Imphal across the grain of the hills of Upper Burma" (2) to cross a river made hazardous by the heavy rains. During this crossing of the river, several men drown, and a subaltern John Ramsay, is badly wounded and later dies. Craig and his remaining men bury him and move toward India.

A year later in an Officers Training School in India, Major Colin Craig is posted as company commander with the specific task of training his cadets "to regain possession of Burma" (5). Among his men is nineteen-year-old R. W. Ramsay, brother of John Ramsay whom Craig had buried in upper Burma. The ghost of John Ramsay dead and buried hovers between them.

R. W. Ramsay at first is not sure if he wants to discuss his dead brother. It is Craig who lays the ground rules. "The thing is that if we don't talk about him you and I will never be able to look at each other without thinking about him. I think that would be a mistake" (7).

They attempt to talk, both ill at ease, more from a need on the part of Craig to explain, to exorcise his feeling of guilt growing out of a sense of personal responsibility for what happened. Haltingly, but carefully selecting his words, Craig explains and admits his failure in not keeping "an eye on John" (9). Craig fervently wants R. W. Ramsay to say it was not his fault. But R. W. Ramsay probes and wants to know if his brother had said anything. "He asked me to finish him off. . . . He bodged the raft . . . he was so weary he just let the men bunch up" (27–28), Craig explains, still feeling keenly responsible for John's death. R. W. Ramsay, who feels the compelling need to say something replies, "I don't feel John's being killed needs any explanation. . . . It was just bad luck really" (29). But the air is not clear in spite of this exchange. The feeling of guilt, of responsibility, haunts and obsesses Craig. The disastrous and tragic event keeps appearing in his sleep, causing him nightmares. The presence of R. W. Ramsay only serves as a constant reminder of that event. With a growing sense of fear and shock Craig realizes that he is actually afraid of R. W. Ramsay. For the truth of the matter is, Craig knows that he was not up to his job. This too he admits to himself "silently into his own darkness" (34).

What went wrong at the river crossing? Is he alone to carry the blame? Given the situation, how would R. W. Ramsay behave? To find the answers to these questions Craig decides to restage that disastrous scene, the crossing of the swollen river. He uses this event as the focal point of the war games he plans, but with one difference. He wants to make it real, not just an exercise.

Craig also wants to use these war games to draw out qualities of dynamic leadership, which he sees in R. W. Ramsay. He, Craig, lacks them, hence the tragedy of the river crossing had occurred, but by bringing out in R. W. Ramsay those qualities he lacked, Craig would be making up for his part in the tragedy. So the war games are both an exorcism of private guilt and a ritualistic initiation into the mystique of leadership.

In Craig's self-doubts about his job, and obsession to train R. W. Ramsay as his better substitute, Scott again interprets his metaphor of man in relationship to his vocation.

Craig wants to train R. W. Ramsay into a leader of men. Train him to make decisions in moments of crisis and not agonize over them afterward. He wants R. W. Ramsay to wear the mark of the warrior so that he will be a man into whose hands the fate of other men can be trusted.

Once the locale has been scouted, it is R. W. Ramsay who devises the scheme for the field exercises. He trains himself for the event with religious fervour. He goes into the jungle to familiarize himself with the forces he has to contend with.

In the war games that follow, R. W. Ramsay acts the tough uncompromising leader. He force marches his men in heat, is rigid in enforcing discipline on the weak ones, and ruthless in making his men stretch to reach their maximum capabilities. He sees in his men "extensions of his own limbs" (132). If they cannot carry through an order he feels it to be a personal affront. He becomes so involved in the simulated war games that he stops playacting. He had developed the instincts of a killer.

This transformation frightens Craig, for that was not his purpose when he set out to initiate R. W. Ramsay into the rituals of leadership. He feels guilty when he realizes that he is "helping Ramsay to destroy himself as a man . . . helping him to be alone in the forest to kill, and that will be the end of him as a man, because that is what man is forbidden" (117).

The games proceed, taking both men and their troops deeper into the forest. R. W. Ramsay has to face the same questions that Craig had to face; what do you do to a wounded man who might slow you and the rest of your troop down? In Craig's case it was John Ramsay. In R. W. Ramsay's case it is a soldier by the name of Everett. "Shoot or leave him? If left, he might live until the enemy found him. Which way? Scream. That way. And death after all. So shoot him now. The last expedient disguised as the last humanity" (131).

The maneuvers move to the crucial crossing of the river. It is to be reenacted the way it had happened a year ago. R. W. Ramsay takes full command. He group forms his men, and displays them strategically. As he organizes this maneuver he senses the possibility of another reason for the death of his brother John.

John bodged the raft on purpose, R. W. Ramsay thinks, and tells Craig "He bodged the raft. He knew what he was doing. He wanted to get rid of the weaklings," and offers the explanation that his brother in bodging the raft had "murdered himself. He couldn't face up to the weak links. He broke the pattern deliberately. He broke his own image" (177). He accuses Craig for not facing up to it but leaving it to John and in the process also killing him. R. W. Ramsay asks Craig if he had "finished him off." Craig does not reply. His silence allows R. W. Ramsay to draw the conclusion that his wounded brother had been left behind to die in agony alone. It increases the tension between the two, and intensifies R. W. Ramsay's desire to do a heroic act to prove to Craig that he, R. W. Ramsay, has the mark of the warrior.

The river crossing takes place, and R. W. Ramsay masterfully guides his men and gets them across, one link after another in the chain, but in midstream, a man misses his footing and another lets go of the raft to help him. Ramsay flounders in to save "not so much the men as the links in the disrupted pattern" (182), and in the process gets caught in the turbulence of the current and dies.

The death of R. W. Ramsay heightens Craig's guilt and sorrow. "I killed him," he confesses to his wife Esther, "It's the only way I can describe my responsibility" (186). Ramsay died trying to save himself, his image, what Craig had made of him, the true warrior or the illusion of the image of the true warrior.

The Mark of The Warrior is a short tightly constructed novel. Although the setting is India, there are no strong identifiable Indian characters except servants and orderlies. The economy of words, the lean athletic prose which often becomes lyrical, particularly in the description of the forest and the river, is reminiscent of Hemingway at his best. There is a biblical simplicity and richness in some of the dialogue.

The world is the world of army cadets, a world that Scott knew well. It is a world of men, of male camaraderie and action. There is just one woman in the novel, Esther, Craig's wife, a minor shadowy figure. But the two main characters—Craig and R. W. Ramsay— emerge fully and believably. The interaction of these two strong personalities provides the dramatic conflict. In their portrayal Scott reveals his ability to analyze the various subtle nuances of character, motive, and action. *The Mark of The Warrior* also makes use, in a minor degree, of narrative techniques that Scott was to use in telling the epic story of *The Raj Quartet.*

In what he calls "The Argument," at the beginning of *The Mark of The Warrior*, Scott articulates his method to create objectivity in telling a story: "Three things are to be considered; a man's estimate of himself, the face he presents to the world, the estimate of that man made by other men. Combined, they form an aspect of truth." It was a method he was to use in creating his many characters in *The Raj Quartet.*

In *The Mark of The Warrior*, a single event which had taken place a year ago, resulting in the death of an individual, is reexamined and seen from the differing view points of Craig and R. W. Ramsay. This technique of varying view points to get at the truth is used impressively and effectively in telling the story of a single event, namely, the rape of an English girl, in *The Raj Quartet.*

The Mark of The Warrior is a serious and sensitive examination of the qualities of leadership and responsibility in men during times of stress. It clearly shows Scott's further development as a novelist. In writing this novel Scott had demonstrated that he could not only write a two-thousand-page novel such as *The Raj Quartet*, but a short compact work of power and beauty as well.

IV   The Birds of Paradise

The Birds of Paradise is "about the man who spent his childhood in India and returned there in a fit of pique because he hated the feeling that he was no more than a consumer of things made by other people. Here the theme of obsession with the need for meaningful occupation, into which the theme of men at work has developed is explicit."[5]

The Birds of Paradise is William Conway's remembrance of things past, recollected in relative tranquillity on Manoba, a pacific island. The time is 1960. But the period covered is from 1919, the year of his birth, to 1960: from the days of the British Raj firmly entrenched on Indian soil to the days of the Raj's decline and disappearance. In viewing the days of his life in retrospect, Conway totally disregards any kind of chronology.

Conway is a London businessman on an expense paid sabbatical. His ten-year marriage resulting in one son (eleven-year-old Stephen) ended in divorce six months ago. He is dissatisfied with his pursuit of the cult of consumerism. To get out of this rut, he wants to go on a sabbatical in some place warm, perhaps in India where he was born. His casual thought is turned into a reality when his firm very efficiently plans the early part of his sabbatical, setting up contacts and itineraries.

Now that he knows he is going East, Conway is anxious to look up Cranston, a Quaker, who had been the prison doctor while a prisoner in Pig Eye, the Japanese POW camp in Malaya. Conway too had been a prisoner there for three and a half years and Cranston, "a one man mobile dispensary" (144), had saved Conway's feet from going gangrenous and had thus saved his life. Conway had not only admired Cranston for his "sense of burning purpose" (146) but had been impressed by his work which was "the only worthwhile thing there was left in the world to do: save life, ease suffering" (146). Conway had sensed something in common with Cranston, "a demon of unrest, a disturbance of the spirit which in his case seemed to have been harnessed to the business of healing the sick"; in Conway's to nothing (147). Cranston loved his job, "it was his life. Without it he might stop breathing" (148). Conway's illusion had been "that a man should love his job, be dedicated to it, born to it" (148), and so when he met Cranston who fitted that image, Conway was attracted to him. Cranston thought of his job as a burnt offering "to be offered up like a sacrifice" (149).

This dedication to his job, Cranston had received from a man called Daintree. Cranston's obsession of and devotion to Daintree reminds us of Tom Brent's obsession with Saxby (*The Love Pavilion*). Daintree worked among the wretched and the forgotten in the backwaters of the world, shoved his flag in isolated communities where no one wanted to go, called them his altars to make *his* burnt offerings.

Conway feels the need to find a purpose to his life, to rediscover the sanctity of a meaningful job, wants spiritual rejuvenation, and is eager to meet Daintree. If Daintree could inspire Cranston, he can inspire Conway too. But only Cranston can tell him the whereabouts of Daintree and so Conway's first stop on his sabbatical is Muzzafirabad, in India.

In Muzzafirabad, Cranston is busily working away planting a different kind of flag on a spread-out map of the world. It is a new Cranston, a far cry from the brutal sadism, and mud and rain-soaked huts, of the prison camp in Pig Eye, where Cranston had stood in pouring rain for four hours to get two aspirin tablets from the Japanese commander for a dying prisoner, and another time when he had submitted himself to the blows of a rattan, which had resulted in brick-red welts on his shoulder, to get some tablets and quinine (147).

Conway learns that Daintree is in Manoba; that he is falling apart by drinking himself to death because "someone had handed him a cure for yaws on a plate, spoiled his old man's dream of a fight to the bitter end" (187) and thus taken away his job, his reason for living. Cranston wants Conway to look up Daintree, be with him, so that he would not die alone (232), and gives Conway a letter of introduction to Daintree.

But before going to Manoba, Conway wants to make a sentimental visit to the source of his childhood happiness, and decides to get in touch with Krishi, his boyhood Indian friend.

Dora Salford, daughter of an English major, Krishi, heir apparent to the princedom of Jundhapur, and Bill Conway, son of the British resident, had been a trio in the halcyon days of the British Raj. They had grown up together in the privileged world of private tutors and governesses and had been waited upon by dutiful and loyal servants.

When Conway gets in touch with Krishi and journeys to Jundhapur he also runs into Dora, who is visiting Krishi. Krishi is now retired and living in the decaying palace on a pension from the Indian government. His wife, Rani, is "living in sin" with a Parsee in Bombay. Dora too is married to Harry Paynter of the Old India Army. It is a nostalgic sentimental reunion, and both Krishi and

Dora share confidences with Conway. They buy him a gift, Melba, a green parrot in a wire cage. They remember the visit they had made to the island in the lake behind the Jundhapur palace. They had rowed out to see the thirty-six birds of paradise inside the cage, beneath the onion-shaped dome suspended "in simulated flight, swooping, hovering and soaring, above the branches and leaves of their natural forest" (75). They make a return visit, but the dead birds are decaying, falling off, for no one is taking care of them, cleaning, mending, brushing them, as old Akbar Ali used to do before his death. Now the cage exudes with the smell of "gum oozing from erectile stalks" (218), of death and decay.

It is Krishi who comments on these birds and thus brings out the symbolism implied in the title *The Birds of Paradise*. The birds in the cage represented the British Raj, "creatures who took it for granted they excited wonder and admiration wherever they went and had no idea that they were dead from the neck up and the neck down, weren't flying at all and were imprisoned in their own conceit anyway" (217). But history had shown that the birds of paradise in the cage were not so much the British Raj, but the princes of India who were dead "in spite of all their finery and high flown postures" and "the British had stuffed them and burnished their fine feathers, but as princes they were dead . . . buried alive in a cage the British had never attempted really to open" (218).

Having completed this return to his childhood days, Conway is even more eager to meet and talk with Daintree, who alone could give his life purpose, or whose end will best illustrate the one he will come to, "for lack of it" (26). This is *the* reason for Conway's stay in Manoba to talk with Daintree, who "Lear-like," and nearly sixty-five, is operating his ramshackle dispensary in a clearing above the plateau. But Conway has to wait for Daintree's mind to clear so that he can talk to him.

During this period of waiting Conway swims and exercises, but "time hangs" heavy on his hands and Conway writes.

He writes about his birth and boyhood in India, in the princedom of Tradura (made up of six princely states), where his father Sir Robert Conway was the representative of the British crown. The Conways had been in India for a long time (like the Brents in *The Love Pavilion* and the Laytons in *The Raj Quartet*) in a tradition of service to the Empire, and young Conway is constantly reminded of his future role to serve the crown, and help Indians lead better lives. It is not his stern and cold father who instills in him the mystique of Empire building, but his governess, Mrs. Canterbury, nicknamed

"Old Mutton," and later his private tutor Grayson-Hume, nick-named "old ho-hum." Grayson-Hume, who kept his homosexual tendencies in check, tells Conway that the British had two jobs in India; to teach democracy to the Indian princes and the art of administration to Indians. Young Bill Conway visualizes for himself a role similar to that of the Romans in Britain.

He grows up with Krishi and Dora and because of his position as the son of the British resident, he has the privilege of celebrating his birthdays by having tea with His Highness, the Maharajah of Tradura. These passages describing his journey in the carriage to the Maha-raja's palace, and his long lonely walk on the persian carpet to Durbar Hall where on the jeweled throne of Tradura sat His Highness with his pulled-down eyes, are replete with realism and humor. The humor is particularly strong when Conway describes how he ate and drank everything in sight, encouraged by His Highness:

"My 'yes, sirs,' and 'no, sirs,' spurted from my swollen mouth with little jets of cake and biscuit crumbs. I fancy there was a high old mess on the floor, but he didn't seem to mind either the mess or the uncontrollable burping brought on by the pop. I sat there, spasmodi-cally galvanised into a position of hunched shoulders, with tightened chest and compressed lips, and with the air puffing out my cheeks and fizzing down my nostrils, and presently wanting very badly to pee: a sensation which when long enough frustrated induced in my face an expression I could feel was idiotic" (38).

At the age of ten, like most Anglo-Indian children, Conway returned to England for his education. He lived with his childless uncle and aunt. But the years in England increased the estrangement between his father and himself.

When Bill Conway is seventeen years old, his father visits him in England and shocks him by suggesting that he ought to go into his uncle's business, and not into Indian service. He had all along visualized an Indian career, and his father's disapproval of such a career shatters young Conway. His father feels that there is no future in India for young Englishmen and by the time he grows up, the only Englishmen in India would be "tourists and commercial travellers" (115). The explanation does not satisfy him. He feels that he has been fooled all these years by being allowed to "act out the part of an old fashioned flag-wagger" (117).

These days of Conway's Anglo-Indian boyhood both in India and England are evoked with sensitivity and understanding, and the prose style matches the pulse and excitement of things remembered.

Childless Uncle Walter leaves him an inheritance, and Conway marries Anne whom he never loved but "couldn't have her any other way" (87). She married him for his money and the possibility of a future knighthood. Both Anne and he are promiscuous, openly and flagrantly, and pursue the life of a consumer with hedonistic abandon. The analysis of their marital problems has all the vitriolic bitchiness of *Who's Afraid of Virginia Woolf* and is reminiscent of the marriage gone sour between Ian Canning and Helen in *A Male Child*, Thornhill and Myra in *The Corrida*, and George and Alice in *The Bender*.

During the war Conway ends up as a prisoner in the Japanese POW camp in Pig Eye in Malaya. It is here he meets Cranston, and hears about Daintree and his burnt offering.

After evacuation from the sadism of Pig Eye he returns to India and journeys to the residency of Gopalakhand to meet his father whom he had not seen since 1936. But they are still strangers to each other.

They play a game of chess one evening. He takes the black pieces and his father the white ones. Within an hour his father's white king faces death, and Conway's black queen gets in at the back and mops up the remaining pawns, one by one, until only the king's knight, is left to defend the monarch. In this defeat of his father Conway sees a subtle yet relevant symbolism. The white pieces were the princely states and all through the years of the British Raj, the crown had stood by them. When independence came to the subcontinent, the princely states, big and small, believed that the crown would guarantee their independent existence. Conway Senior believed in it too. But in this chess game where only the king's knight (namely, Conway Senior) was left to defend the monarch (namely, the Maharajah of Gopalakhand) Conway Junior sees "it all prophetically written" (163).

After this brief period of rest and rehabilitation in India Conway returns to England to join uncle Walter's business. From this vantage point Conway watches the end of the Raj, the end of the world of the Maharajahs, and the end of his father who stays on in India retiring to a place called Dhooni in the hills to write his memoirs, where he dies.

Conway had wanted to contribute to human society by serving the Empire. But the Empire was gone. He had regained a spark of service when he assisted Cranston in the sickness and brutality of Pig Eye, but when he returned to London he merely ended up as a taker, a consumer. Now he is in Manoba, and all he can do is to watch Daintree die, after which he, Conway, will return to London. It is as though he is always there to see the ends that people come to.

In a fascinating account, one of the richer sections of the novel, in a blend of history, myth, and legend, Conway recounts the story of the fabled birds of paradise. The bird of paradise was a footless bird, as indicated in its Latin name: *Paradisea Apoda*. As children, all three of them, Conway, Krishi, and Dora had been fascinated by the birds in the cage. To Conway it was their color and finery; to Krishi, the secret joke that the stuffed birds of paradise were really the British; to Dora, "omens of all the marvellous things that were going to happen later" (223).

In this metaphor of the birds of paradise, Conway sees his obsession, the end that people come to. His recollections, "these days of my life in retrospect" (182), is really about ends. The end of the colorful, romantic and grandiose Empire; the end of a dream of service to that Empire as in the case of Conway; the end of the proud, magnificent princes who had nursed the illusion of staying on forever; the ignoble end of Senior Conway who did not know when to end his career; the end of Daintree; and the end too of that Cranston who had found his altar in the most wretched places for his burnt offering. And in the bird of paradise with its legs cut off Conway sees the deeper symbolism of the mutilation of the Indian subcontinent, limbs torn asunder, into two nations, India and Pakistan: the end of one nation.

It is in these various shades of meaning that *The Birds of Paradise* can be called a "rich" novel. It is not so much crafted as composed. The rhythms of life, of people, and of nations, moves from the idyllic childhood, with tones of subtle sadness, anguish, and estrangement, to alienation and longing in London. Then the tone and rhythm changes to the clanging, fervent, fevered percussion of marital bitterness and frantic pursuit of hedonistic pleasure. Then to the drumlike beat to evoke the funereal sadness and brutality of Pig Eye; to wistful nostalgia on the sentimental journey to India concluding with rhythms of tranquillity in Manoba.

The Birds of Paradise foreshadows *The Raj Quartet*. After its publication in 1962, Scott's next work was *The Jewel in the Crown* (1966), the first volume in *The Raj Quartet*. Sir William Conway reappears in *The Raj Quartet*, and his advice to his Maharajah not to accede to India or Pakistan, which is but a paragraph in one of the history books referred to in *The Birds of Paradise*, is the subject of a long editorial in the fourth volume of *The Raj Quartet* (*A Division of the Spoils*). The casually mentioned locale of Pankot becomes an important and clearly mapped out locale particularly in the second volume of *The Raj Quartet* (*The Day of the Scorpion*) and *the* locale in Scott's last novel, *Staying On*. The powerful metaphor implied in

The Towers of Silence, which becomes the title of the third volume of *The Raj Quartet*, is already in Scott's mind in *The Birds of Paradise* as he makes a reference to both the towers and the waiting vultures. There is but a casual reference to the existence of defectors to the Indian National Army in *The Birds of Paradise*. This theme is developed elaborately in *The Raj Quartet*.

When we read the passage in *The Birds of Paradise* describing Conway's "gesture to the food" by not allowing "anything going to waste because it had earned the right not to be squandered" (130), an attitude he has developed after his POW experiences, we read of a similar passage in the fourth volume of *The Raj Quartet* (*A Division of the Spoils*). Colonel John Layton is returning home after his years as a POW in Europe and reveals the same careful attitude toward waste of any scrap of food. In fact, the entire rehabilitation experience of Conway in his father's house in Gopalakhand has echoes in the passages describing the train journey bringing Colonel Layton home to Pankot.

But in a more central way *The Birds of Paradise* states the theme, "the ends that people come to," that Scott was going to explore more fully in *The Raj Quartet*. In describing the town of Ranpur, in the second volume of *The Raj Quartet* (*The Day of The Scorpion*), he speaks of the British coming "to the end of themselves as they were."

From the discursiveness and lack of control exhibited in *The Chinese Love Pavilion*, Scott returns to control and mastery of his vast material in *The Birds of Paradise*, an excellent and necessary introduction to *The Raj Quartet*.

CHAPTER 6

The Raj Quartet *as Story*

THE RAJ QUARTET is one of the masterpieces of twentieth-century English literature. It is the quintessential achievement of Paul Scott who devoted ten years of his life to write "one of the longest and most successfully executed works of nineteenth century fiction written in the twentieth century."[1]

The Raj Quartet was not originally conceived as a four-volume work, and the volumes themselves were published separately between 1965 and 1975 as *The Jewel in the Crown, The Day of the Scorpion, The Towers of Silence*, and *A Division of the Spoils*. But *The Quartet*—as it will be referred to for convenience—must be considered as a single work to experience the total impact, and the unified literary and artistic achievement that it represents. The publication of the four volumes in one in 1977 not only emphasizes the interlocking unity of the volumes but makes it possible to read, enjoy, and study them as a single work.

The Raj Quartet is so called because "Raj" means "rule," means "kingdom," "means power and glory of the ruler. To English people it means a phase in their imperial history."[2] To Indians it meant the Englishman who represented the British government, and sometimes it meant any Englishman.

Hence the collective title *The Raj Quartet* for the total work, because *The Quartet* covers the last five years of British rule in India (1942–1947), from the Japanese invasion to Indian independence, from the beginnings of the Raj's decline to its disappearance.

The Quartet works on several levels of time and space sequences. It is structured intricately with "rhythms" of its own interlocking the volumes. It is almost two thousand pages, more than half a million words, and a vast canvas on which some three hundred and seventy characters play out their roles.

How to deal with such a work raises several questions. As *The Quartet* begins to gain an increasing audience of students and scholars it will be mined endlessly for various studies of themes, techniques, imagery, plots and subplots, characters and their originals—real and imagined.

In this study *The Quartet* will be considered from four perspectives: as story; as novel; as history; and as a study in race and class distinctions. This chapter will review volume by volume, to provide a framework of reference, of story line and major characters, to aid in understanding the total work.

I   The Jewel in the Crown

The theme of *The Quartet* is explicitly stated in the first volume. "This is the story of a rape, of the events that led up to it and followed it and of the place in which it happened" (*J,* 1).[3] The rape, the Bibighar affair, took place on the night of August 9, 1942, in the Bibighar Gardens in Mayapore. Twenty years later, the narrator of this story who describes himself as the Stranger, has returned to Mayapore to conduct a personal investigation of this crime. He wants to reexamine the evidence because even after this period of time there has been "a trial of sorts going on" (*J,* 1), and because "a specific historical event has no definite ending, no satisfactory end" (*J,* 119).

The Stranger's interest in the case is the result of his scholarly involvement in this period of British Indian history and his reading of an unpublished book dealing with the Bibighar affair by Brigadier A. V. Reid who had been in Mayapore at the time of the crime (*J,* 312).

Like an investigative journalist the Stranger retraces the events leading to the rape. He visits places and talks to people who had been involved in this case neither directly or indirectly. To get at the truth of the matter he also examines entries from diaries, unpublished memoirs, extracts from private journals, and correspondence. He presents his findings by allowing each fragment of evidence to articulate its point of view. He does not intrude. He sets the stage, turns on the lights, and introduces the catalytic events leading up to the incident under scrutiny.

Unfortunately, the three main figures involved in the Bibighar affair cannot be interviewed. Daphne, the raped English girl, is dead; Hari Kumar, the young Anglicized Indian accused of the crime, has gone "into oblivion, probably changing his name once more" (*J,* 71); and Ronald Merrick, the superintendent of police who had pursued this case with singleminded obsession, seems "to be lost, temporarily at least, in the anonymity of time or other occupation" (*J,* 71).

Another event of equal horror and tragedy, although not of such political and emotional significance as the Bibighar affair, "the key to the whole situation" (*J*, 59), had taken place earlier on the same day. A fifty-seven-year-old English woman, Edwina Crane, had been crudely beaten and an Indian school teacher, D. R. Chaudhuri, brutally murdered. Crane cannot be interviewed because she had committed suicide.

The Stranger therefore begins with Lady Lili Chatterjee in whose residence, the impressive MacGregor House, he is a "house guest" (*J*, 158). Lady Chatterjee, wife of late Sir Nello Chatterjee, is a member of the upper-class Indian society. She and her late husband had been on intimate terms with the Manners, the late Sir George and Lady Ethyl, uncle and aunt of Daphne.

But before Lady Chatterjee begins to talk about the Bibhigar affair, the Stranger comments on the historical catalyst that resulted in the above violent events.

The Indians have lost faith in their rulers, the British. Instead of the promised freedom and increasing participation in the government there has been greater repression. Without even the gesture of a consultation with any of the Indian nationalist leaders, India has been dragged into a war. Gandhi and the Congess Party, disillusioned by these acts, have passed the "Quit India" resolution, serving notice on the British to leave India to God or to anarchy—but go! The Japanese have invaded Burma and have plans for liberating India from colonial oppression. The arrest and imprisonment of Gandhi and other Indian leaders only adds to the explosive situation.

Edwina Crane, superintendent of the district's Protestant Mission Schools, a long time admirer of Gandhi and supporter of Indian aspirations, is disillusioned by this recent act of her hero. She removes his photograph from her study and stops entertaining Indian ladies to tea. She has been in India for thirty-five of her fifty-seven years, having come out with a British family, the Nesbitt-Smiths, as travel companion to their two children. When they leave for home after three years, she stays on, taking a job as teacher at the Joseph Wainwright Christian School, a privately endowed school for the children of mixed parentage.

Gandhi's picture comes down but another picture, which she had received as a gift in 1914, stays on the wall. This is a semiallegorical picture showing Queen Victoria in all her regal splendor surrounded by representative figures of her Indian Empire; Mr. Disraeli, her prime minister, proudly showing her a map of her dominion, and an

Indian prince offering her a sparkling jewel on a cushion, the brightest jewel in the crown of the empress which was India herself. The title and the metaphor for this first volume is derived from this picture.

Crane, who has mixed feelings about the picture, is, however, certain of one thing, "India *must* be independent. When the war's over we've got to give her up" (*J*, 35). But for the present she looks upon the coming together of India and England "as equal partners in a war to the death against totalitarianism" (*J*, 35), as the only hope of avoiding civil uprisings and bitterness.

On the morning of August 8, 1942, Crane sets out in her old Ford on a school visit to Dibrapur. She dismisses rumors of impending trouble and words of caution by her fifty-year-old servant Joseph, for she is a tough old bird.

In Dibrapur she meets the Indian teacher, Mr. D. R. Chaudhuri, but because he is a "sensitive Indian who knew the English language, even some of its subtlest nuances" (*J*, 41), she has to be meticulous in her selection of words but realizes that "when you chose your words the spontaneity went out of the things you wanted to say" (*J*, 41).

Violence is in the air and the safety of the school is threatened. So next morning Crane and Chaudhuri on their way to find a refuge for the children are confronted by rioters who crowd around Crane's car. Chaudhuri is dragged out and he urges Crane to go but she hesitates, and to get her moving he taunts her, "Do you only take orders from white men?" (*J*, 56). She gets out of the hostile crowd and watches with horror and helplessness as Chaudhuri is beaten to death by the rioters. She drags his dead body to a side, and sits in the pouring rain holding his hand.

Crane is found by one of the British officials, hospitalized, and slowly recovers, but does not identify any of the assailants. "Being fair at all costs to the bloody blacks" (*J*, 58), is the verdict passed on her by the Anglo-Indian community of Mayapore. Crane is emotionally shattered, for her dream of Britain leaving India peacefully now proves to have been an illusion. She removes the portrait of the queen, the jewel in her crown, from the wall in her study. In this mood of dark melancholy she dresses herself in a white saree, the flag of her adopted country India, and sets fire to herself in the act of *suttee*.[4]

Lady Chatterjee knew Crane casually. She had met her at one of the parties given by Robin White, the deputy commissioner of Mayapore, where Crane had drunk everything she had been offered: "Sherry, white burgundy, claret and brandy" (*J*, 30). While Lady

Chatterjee has no use for Crane's wooly-headed do-gooder attitude, she admires physical courage, which is "usually informed by moral courage too" (*J*, 68). Lady Chatterjee, however, knew Daphne very well. Daphne had been doing some volunteer work at the local hospital and had stayed with her in MacGregor House. From Lady Chatterjee we get a picture of Daphne as, a big, rather clumsy girl, with weak eyes "always dropping things" (*J*, 71), to whom "India was a thing" (*J*, 87). She had been born in the Punjab but had gone home as a child because her mother could not stand India.

To supplement her picture of Daphne, Lady Chatterjee takes the Stranger to Daphne's room and lets him take "possession" of it, to feel the atmosphere, see her photograph, look and touch objects she had handled. Because Lady Chatterjee is convinced of the genuineness of the Stranger's interest in the Bibighar affair, she gives him two letters of Daphne's written to her aunt Lady Ethel Manners. Toward the end of this volume we learn that Lady Chatterjee had also given the Stranger excerpts of Daphne's journal pertaining to the Bibighar affair.

The two letters—long, chatty, sentimental, gossipy—introduce the three other characters in *The Quartet*: Ronald Merrick, Hari Kumar, and Sister Ludmila.

Merrick is a bachelor, "fair haired, blue eyed and awfully good looking" (*J*, 99). Daphne meets him at a party, and one of the first things Merrick warns her is to keep away from Kumar. She enjoys "the best English-style meal" she has had in India at Merrick's bungalow and he proposes to her. She thanks him for the proposal "but." In her second and last letter she promises to tell her aunt about Hari Kumar, who has just been a name in these letters, and about Sister Ludmila, who "wears nun's clothing and collects dead bodies" (*J*, 103). The following day Lady Chatterjee fills the Stranger in on Hari Kumar, about whom she has mixed feelings, for he had "too big a chip on his shoulder" (*J*, 106), and briefly on Sister Ludmila, about whom she had "a horror" (*J*, 108).

Hari Kumar's father wanted to mold his son into as close a facsimile of an Englishman as possible. He changed his son's name to Harry Coomer to make it sound more British. He educated and trained his son in England to speak and think like an English boy, but his skin however, remained brown and did not turn white. With the death of his father Kumar had to return to India where the color of his skin became his badge of doom in British India. He met Daphne and their friendship turned to love which unfortunately spelled danger in British India, which did not look favorably upon such fraternization between members of the two races, the ruler and the ruled, white and black.

On the troubled and politically charged night of August 9, Daphne and Kumar had gone out to be by themselves in the Bibighar Gardens. They had walked, talked, made love, and were relaxing when five or six Indian assailants invaded their privacy and raped Daphne.

Sister Ludmila,[5] of obscure origins but called sister by the Indians, and whose business was with the dying and not the dead (J, 123), had met both Kumar and Daphne on separate occasions in the Sanctuary, her place of work where she brought the dying "to reach and warm the cold diminishing centre of the departing soul" (J, 123). The Sanctuary is now an orphanage and the Stranger, walking the very paths that Sister Ludmila had walked in her ministry of the sick, "looking like some pre-historic bird miraculously risen" (J, 114), calls on her to talk to her about Kumar and Daphne.

Sister Daphne is old and blind and bedridden, but her memory of Kumar and Daphne is fresh and vivid. She also remembers Merrick when he had come to the Sanctuary looking for Kumar. She had met Kumar several times and believes he treated her as a mother-confessor (J, 247), talking to her about his English friend, Colin Lindsey. Kumar had also written an article about Sister Ludmila for the *Mayapore Gazette,* but the editor had refused to publish it "because of the implication that the British were responsible for letting people die in the streets" (J, 384). Ludmila had found Kumar drunk and lying on the road on one of her rounds, before the Bibighar affair. With the help of her associate, Mr. deSouza, she had brought him to the Sanctuary. She recalls Kumar's dark handsomeness. She remembers Merrick who had come soon after to pick up Kumar for questioning, surreptitiously watching Kumar's muscular beauty. She observes that Kumar, who spoke no Indian language, spoke English "better accented than Merrick's" (J, 129), which immediately counted against Kumar in Merrick's book. Merrick was also aware that Kumar and Daphne were friends and that this too counted against Kumar, for Merrick was fond of Daphne and had wanted to marry her.

Daphne had called on Sister Ludmila after the Bibighar affair and had told her that she would not abort the child, Kumar's child, even though people of her race had told her to do so "like a duty" (J, 146).

Daphne had no knowledge of where Kumar was, in what prison, and her attempts to find out had been futile. She had not identified her five or six assailants except to say that "they could have been British soldiers with their faces blacked like commandos" (*J*, 150). Ludmila concludes by saying that it took courage on the part of Daphne to make such unorthodox comments during those times.

The Mayapore Club is the next stop for the Stranger. He goes with Lady Chatterjee to meet Srinivasan, an Indian lawyer who proves to be a helpful source of information on the Bibighar affair. In his rambling manner, he talks about the history of the Mayapore Club and brings to the attention of the Stranger an important document, the Club Members' Book for 1939-1945. Examining it the Stranger sees "the curiously rounded and child like" (*J*, 175) Merrick's signature and Daphne's name as his guest. He also notices the signature of a Captain Colin Lindsey as "a temporary privileged member" (*J*, 175).

The signature of Colin Lindsey in the Club Members' Book provides a convenient point for the Stranger to fill us in on Kumar's background.

Colin Lindsey was Kumar's closest friend. He had grown up with him in Didbury, had studied together in Chillingborough, and shared hopes and dreams for the future. When Kumar's father Duleep Kumar, who had preferred to be called David, died bankrupt in Edinburgh of an overdose of sleeping pills, Kumar turned to Colin's parents for help and comfort. But when they found out that Kumar's father's financial empire had been built on shady deals, even a possible case of forgery, they grew cold and distant. Kumar had no other choice but to return to India. His passage was paid for by his aunt Shalini, his father's favorite sister. His father had wanted desperately to gain for Kumar an "entrance into a society that stood beyond his . . . natural reach" (*J*, 219).

At eighteen years, Kumar had returned to the land of his birth, an alien. "His sharpest memories were of piles of leaves, wet and chill to the touch, as if in early morning after a late October frost" (*J*, 220). Living in Chillianwallah Bagh, the Indian section of Mayapore, and uncomfortable in the confined quarters of his aunt, Kumar hungered for letters from Colin. When they had arrived he had become even more aware of the sharp pain of his exile. But he never shared this pain with his friend, never once told him of the suffocation he was enduring in the "tight, closed, pseudo-orthodox Hindu society . . . the acquisitive middle-class merchant India of money under the floorboards, and wheat and rice hoarded up until there is a famine somewhere and you can off-load it at a handsome profit, even if most of it has gone bad" (*J*, 225–226). But he had resolved to himself to become an Indian the English would welcome and recognize. "His father's death had raised the question of moral indebtedness" (*J*, 227). After a casual visit to a pharmacy in the British or cantonment section of the town, where he was rudely insulted, he had sadly realized that however English he might be, as an Indian with brown skin he had become "invisible to white people" (*J*, 235), and that his father's plans had been built on an illusion and that in India "an Indian and an Englishman could never meet on equal terms" (*J*, 241).

Through lawyer Srinivasan the Stranger learns some more facts about Hari: that Hari had tried to learn Hindi from an Indian teacher Pandit Baba Sahib, but had abandoned it; that for a while he had worked for his uncle; that he had seriously tried to get a position with the firm of British-Indian Electrical Company which would have given him a chance to return to England for some advanced training; that Kumar had fallen foul of the Englishman who had interviewed him; that Kumar's superior English and the fact that he had not behaved submissively enough for an Indian, had lost him the job and earned him the epithet of an arrogant bolshie black lad; that Kumar had ended up as a free-lance reporter for the *Mayapore Gazette*.

B. V. Laxminarayan had been editor at that time, and the Stranger calls on him. He is contemptuous of Kumar, calling him, "a lickspittle of the Raj" (*J*, 246), because of his English manners and accent and had shown no interest in helping him when Kumar had been in trouble.

Kumar had continued his correspondence with Colin but had begun to notice a change of tone in Colin's letters. It is with Sister Ludmila that Hari had talked about Colin. Colin had joined the army and had written from "somewhere in France" and later as part of the India Command from Meerut in India, Colin had continued his correspondence. Finally Kumar had glimpsed Colin in Mayapore. He had rushed home to see if there had been a letter from him, telling him he was in Mayapore and asking where and when they could meet. There was no such letter, and Kumar had made excuses for Colin by thinking that the man he had glimpsed was probably not Colin. But it was Colin, for Kumar had seen him close enough at a flower show which he had attended as a reporter for the *Mayapore Gazette*. Colin had looked at him, "and then away without recognition, not understanding that in those *babu* clothes, under the bazaar topee, there was one black face he ought to have seen as being different from the rest" (*J*, 262).

This, above all else since his return to India, had proved to be the shattering experience. Kumar had found in this rejection by his closest friend the incontrovertible confirmation of his earlier opinion that he was indeed invisible to white people in India; to all white people, both strangers and friends. It was on the night of Colin's rejection that Kumar had gone but for the first time with some Indians and got totally drunk. He had passed out on the road, and had been picked up by Sister Ludmila, and had then come face to face with Ronald Merrick and ended up as his victim, for Anglicized, educated Kumar posed a threat to Merrick's own deep sense of insecurity and humble English origins. Also, by his dark handsomeness Kumar had stirred Merrick's repressed homosexual desires. Since Merrick could not love him he chose to hate him.

The Stranger at this stage in his narration inserts the "Edited Extracts from the Unpublished Memoirs of Brigadier A. V. Reid, DSO, MC: *A Simple Life*, the document which had aroused the Stranger's interest in the Bibighar affair.

Brigadier Reid was in Mayapore as head of the Indian Infantry Brigade at the time of the Bibighar affair. Reid's is the official military view of the Bibighar affair.

Reid (whose name turned around means Dyer, the man responsible for the infamous Jallianwallah Bagh Massacre in 1919)[6] is a firm believer in the mystique of the Empire, a hard-liner who considered Gandhi and his ideas "the impractical dreams of a man who believed that everyone was—or should be—as simple and innocent as himself" (*J*, 269). He recited Kipling's poetry to inspire men of his battalion to go out and do the job. While he dislikes Robin White, the deputy commissioner whom he characterizes as pro-Indian, Reid takes an instant liking to Ronald Merrick (who in physical appearance reminds him of his only son Alan who had died working on the infamous Burma-Siam Railway).

It is Merrick who informs Reid of Daphne's rape in the Bibighar Gardens and the discovery of Daphne's bicycle, stolen by one of the culprits, "in a ditch outside a house in Chillianwallah Bagh" (*J*, 288). This is an important piece of evidence, and we will see as *The Quartet* progresses the significant part played by the bicycle evidence. Merrick characterizes Kumar as an undesirable character who had somehow cast a spell over Daphne.

The Stranger sends Reid's document to Robin White who was

deputy commissioner of Mayapore at that time, for his reactions, along with a list of several new questions.

The Stranger inserts White's comments on Reid's document, on Daphne's journals, and on the deposition made by Vidyasagar, one of the suspects in the Bibighar affair. We also get the unedited journals of Daphne's and Vidyasagar's deposition to assist us in finding the truth and solve the mystery of the Bibighar affair.

White did not know Kumar, and from what he has heard he thinks him a conundrum (*J*, 331). But of Merrick, White says that he "was killed during the communal riots that attended partition" (*J*, 311) of India in 1947.

White characterizes the drama that he and Reid played out as a "conflict between Englishmen who liked and admired Indians and believed them capable of self-government, and Englishmen who disliked or feared or despised them" (*J*, 315). On the British in India White offers the opinion, "We were in India for what we could get out of it" (*J*, 317) and thoughtfully meditates on the long history of British Indian relations.

"A Deposition by Vidyasagar" introduced by the Stranger is written in a style of English that an Indian might use. Vidyasagar tells the story of his early life which was one of "shame and wickedness, going with loose women and impairing" his health (*J*, 334). But when he casually comes across an Indian Christian teacher who opens up to him a world of books and reading, Vidyasagar moves forward to a life of political awareness. He begins associating with politically oriented young men and follows with interest the formation of the Indian National Army by the Indian nationalist Subhas Chandra Bose. Bose's purpose to "liberate" India with the help of the Japanese ignites the deep-seated patriotism in Vidyasagar and his associates. They get involved in underground political pamphleteering.

Vidyasagar knew Kumar, casually at first, and had gone out drinking with him the night Kumar had become "invisible" to Colin. Because the police discovered his underground political printing activities, Vidyasagar had been arrested, tortured, and sentenced to two years rigorous imprisonment.

After Vidyasagar's release he learns from a friend of his, one of the boys arrested in connection with the Bibighar affair, by the name of Sharma (a pseudonym), of what had happened to him and others in prison, including Kumar. Merrick had examined Sharma's private parts in the police station and titillatingly interrogated him about happenings in the Bibighar Gardens on the night of the rape. Sharma also tells Vidyasagar that he had been allowed to see Kumar in a dimly lit room, "naked, fastened over one of the iron trestles" (*J*, 347), and that there was blood on his buttocks and that Kumar had been beaten and was experiencing great difficulty in breathing. The police had wanted Kumar to believe that Sharma had confessed and implicated him so as to break Kumar and force a confession out of him, a confession that he had raped Daphne. Sharma had shouted out to Kumar that he had told nothing to the police because he knew nothing. Sharma and his friends had been given food in prison, and it is only after they had eaten were they told by their Muslim jailors that they had eaten beef and that as Hindus they were now outcasts.

The Stranger now introduces Daphne's journals written "to help her understand things better and as an insurance against permanent silence" (*J*, 349). Daphne wrote in Kashmir, during her pregnancy, awaiting the birth of her child. In her journal she tells her aunt that she had not been a virgin prior to the Bibighar affair, but that Kumar was the only man she loved. She is sad because she has no hope of seeing him again and hence the child is very important to her. She thinks it will be a boy. While she hopes the child will resemble Kumar, she has "nightmares of the child growing up to resemble no one, black-skinned beyond redemption, a creature of the dark, a tiny living mirror of that awful night" (*J*, 365).

In great detail Daphne writes about her first meeting with Kumar and of his background; and the visits to the Hindu temple of Tirupathi.

They went to the Bibighar Gardens because they had wanted privacy. There they had made love and were lying half asleep when her rapists had come upon them. After the violent act she had seen Kumar. They had "bound his hands and mouth and ankles with strips of cloth" (*J*, 407), and had placed him in a position "where he would have had to close his eyes if he didn't want to see what was happening" (*J*, 407).

She had crawled over to him and freed him, extracting a promise from him to say that he had been at home, that they had never seen each other that day. She then dragged herself out of the Bibighar Gardens.

Interspersed with this minute report about the rape are her feelings about India and Britain. She sees in her rape a larger symbol, another rape by Britain, "not in malice. Perhaps there was love. Oh, somewhere in the past. . . . But the spoilers are always there" (*J*, 434).

Through the letters of Lady Manners written to Lady Chatterjee, which the Stranger now attaches at the conclusion of Daphne's journal, we learn that Daphne had given birth to a girl and in the process died of peritonitis. The child, sweet and pretty, named Parvathi, would be brought up as an Indian, and Lady Manners entrusts her upbringing to Lady Chatterjee after she has gone. Lady Manners is heartbroken at the division of India, "The creation of Pakistan is our crowning failure" (*J*, 444).

The Stranger departs after proper good-byes to Lady Chatterjee and to young Parvathi who lives with her. Parvathi is a lovely young girl, devoted to the study of Indian music which her English mother Daphne had described as "the only music in the world [which] sounded conscious of breaking silence and going back into it when it was finished" (*J*, 451).

Thus concludes the first volume of *The Quartet* with "always the promise of a story continuing instead of finishing" (*J*, 450).

II The Day of the Scorpion

The second volume of *The Quartet* covers the period between 1942 and 1944, and "The Stranger" of *The Jewel in the Crown* describes himself here as "The Writer" (*S*, 1), and then reverts back to calling himself "The Stranger" (*S*, 3). Some of the characters from *The Jewel* reappear, notably Hari Kumar—about whose whereabouts everyone seemed to be in doubt as *The Jewel* concluded—and Ronald Merrick. Either new information is given—of Hari Kumar, that he is in the Kandipat jail—or the characters are seen from another point of view and hence take on an added depth and an even greater sense of mystery as in the case of Ronald Merrick. Even a walk-on character such as Pandit Baba, Kumar's short term Hindu teacher in *The Jewel*, emerges in *The Scorpion* as a full-fledged personality, a devious politician belonging to the fanatical brand of Hindu nationalism.

New characters are introduced, notably Mohammed Ali Kasim and his two sons. We get acquainted with a new English family, the Laytons, and they dominate the novel, particularly one of the girls, Sarah Layton. Count Bronowski, chief minister of Mirat, and the ruler of Mirat are new creations in *The Scorpion*. Barbara Batchelor, who will dominate the third volume of *The Quartet*, *The Towers of Silence*, and Lucy Smalley, who not only emerges with new insights in *The Towers* but takes center stage in *Staying On*, Paul Scott's last novel, also make their initial appearance in *The Scorpion*.

Mayapore was the locale in *The Jewel*, but in *The Scorpion* new locales such as Ranpur, Pankot, and the princely State of Mirat become parts of the geography of *The Quartet*.

The main theme of *The Quartet*, the rape of Daphne in the Bibighar Gardens, is of course ever present, sometimes aggressively conspicuous, other times hovering in the background, but always in the wings, alert and ready to make its presence felt. It haunts people and places. It is viewed from different perspectives, and while we had Daphne's version of it in *The Jewel* through her journals, in *The Scorpion* we have Hari Kumar's version.

In *The Jewel* the Raj was on the decline. In *The Scorpion* it is disappearing. In *The Jewel* Edwina Crane had removed the splendorous imperial portrait of the jewel in her crown as if preparing to pack it in and cart it away to some museum as a dead historical piece. In *The Scorpion* the metaphor of the beseiged and disappearing Raj is sought in the image of the scorpion which, when circled by fire, stings itself to death, representing the death wish of persons and the race.

The Stranger has returned to Ranpur—which used to be predominantly Muslim before the partition—to trace the realities of the Bibighar affair, for in places like Ranpur, "the British came to the end of themselves as they were" (*S*, 3).

The story begins with the arrest of Mohammed Ali Kasim, MAK to newspapers and Mac to the British. His arrest is part of a nationwide arrest of nationalist leaders on the aftermath of the "Quit India" resolution which was the historical catalyst in *The Jewel*. MAK is a man of culture and sophistication, and could trace his genealogy back to an ancestor who had intermarried with a Hindu girl under the great Moghul Akbar, who had dreamed of a united India of Hindus and Muslims. He was now going to prison for that dream of a united India.

MAK is taken to the Fort in Premnagar. It is from Major Tippit, who is in charge of the Fort, that MAK hears about Daphne, "that poor girl," and Crane, "that unfortunate woman" (*S*, 27). Through newspapers MAK learns about the death of Daphne and the birth of Parvathi. He writes a letter to Governor Malcolm and also to Lady Manners. In MAK's letter to the governor is telescoped and summarized the Bibighar affair. Thus, the story is brought up to date for the reader not familiar with *The Jewel*. The link is established and continuity developed in *The Scorpion*.

MAK has two sons, Sayed and Ahmed. Sayed, his elder son, holds the king-emperor's commission and is in the army, but at the time of the story he is a POW of the Japanese. The Japanese use MAK's arrest to disillusion Sayed about his loyalties to the British, and Sayed joins the Indian National Army (INA). When the Japanese use the INA units to move into India, Sayed, who is now a major in the INA, is captured by the British in Manipur. The news of his capture is given to MAK by his son Ahmed toward the end of *The Scorpion* when MAK is released from prison.

This turn of events, namely, the king's soldiers going to fight the king's wars and returning as king's prisoners, has a frightening impact on British morale. The Indian army "was the finest army in the world. Subvert it and it could turn and destroy its creators like a man swatting flies" (*S*, 166). This theme keeps recurring in *The Scorpion* and contributes to the overall feeling that the Raj is not just declining, it is disappearing.

MAK's second son Ahmed, a bit of a playboy, who according to an Englishwoman would make a good maitre d' if he did not stink so abominably of garlic, is currently social secretary to Count Bronowski, the chief minister of Mirat. Ahmed, who seems superficial, rises to heroic stature by his magnanimous gesture of personal sacrifice in the fourth and final volume of *The Quartet, A Division of the Spoils.* From the Kasim family our attention is shifted to the English family of the Laytons.

The Laytons had been in India for a long time. "Bone of India's bone" (*S*, 343), generations of Laytons had served king and queen, administering justice, and fighting wars and representing the essence of *Man-bap* ("I am your Father and your Mother") to Indian soldiers. In creating the Laytons, and intricately and believably tracing and linking their many branches of the family tree, in England, India, and then back in England, Paul Scott has written a novel within a novel. In their origins, rise, and fall we see mirrored the fortunes and disasters of the Empire itself and gain a deeper understanding of the life of the Raj.

Ranpur was the permanent cool weather station for the Laytons and Pankot a hill station for the summer. Pankot was thoroughly English. "There were English people who said they were reminded of the Surrey hills near Caterham" (*S*, 54).

Two of the Layton children, Sarah and Susan, were born in Pankot. Their father, John Frederick William Layton, was married here. Their grandfather, James Layton, had served as deputy commissioner for Pankot District.

John Layton of Chillingborough (the same school Kumar and

Colin Lindsey had been to) lost his mother quite early and had dim memories of her. When his father James Layton married again, his stepmother Mabel became more of a mother to him than his own mother had been. John Layton marries Mildred Muir, daughter of another "India family." Their marriage produces two daughters, Sarah and Susan, born in 1921 and 1922 respectively. "Sarah was her father's daughter while Susan was her mother's" (*S*, 55). It is Sarah who dominates the scene in *The Scorpion*.

Susan's wedding, widowhood, birth of child, and withdrawal into a silent world of melancholy is an important theme in *The Scorpion*.[7]

Mildred Layton, the mother, whose husband is a POW in Germany, has discreetly begun to overindulge with the bottle, and her promiscuous behavior and hostility toward her daughter, Sarah, symptomatic in *The Scorpion*, intensifies in the third volume of *The Quartet*, *The Towers of Silence*.

Then there is her step–mother-in-law, Mabel Layton, mistress of Rose Cottage, a strong independent woman who already senses that the days of the Raj are over. She had refused to be identified with the group of Britishers raising funds for General Dyer, who had been responsible for the massacre at Jallianwallah Bagh. Instead, Mabel Layton had sent a check to Sir Ahmed Akbar Aki Kasim, father of MAK, to help the Indian families who had been hurt by the massacre. As she grows old the memory of Jallianwallah Bagh grows strong and fearful, and she is troubled by the collective guilt of her race which she expresses in her troubled sleep: Jallianwallah Bagh comes out garbled as Gillian Waller. Mabel Layton emerges more fully in the third volume of *The Quartet*, *The Towers of Silence*, where by her very withdrawal into her rose garden she precipitates action and conflict.

The Scorpion, then, introduces these four, fascinatingly complex, Layton women.

The Laytons are busy preparing for Susan's wedding as their part of the story begins in *The Scorpion*. In addition, a group of Indians under the probable direction of Pandit Baba Sahib are planning to create an incident at the wedding, the reason being the presence of Ronald Merrick, who by sheer accident has stepped into the role of best man at the wedding.

The wedding is to take place in Mirat, "barely more than the size of a pocket handkerchief" (*S*, 146), an independent princely state whose ruler is His Highness Nawab Sir Ahmed Ali Gaffur Kasim Bahadur of the House of Kasim. The Nawab had brought to Mirat Count

Bronowski from Monte Carlo to whom he had said, "make me modern" (S, 93).

Bronowski, seventy years old, with a lame left leg and a blind left eye covered by a black patch, the result of a bomb thrown in his direction "in pre-revolutionary St. Petersburg by an anarchist while driving along Nevsky Prospect to the Winter Palace" (S, 84), is a homosexual. But he realizes that his object of desire, Ahmed Kasim, is unattainable and therefore he checks his hunger. His influence over the Nawab is complete. He has transformed Mirat from a feudal autocracy to a semidemocratic state.

In introducing Bronowski and the princely State of Mirat, Paul Scott introduces and elaborates on another significant strand in the tapestry of the Raj, the relationship of the princes and their dilemma when the Raj disappeared. It is a theme he had dealt with earlier in *The Birds of Paradise* and to a minor extent in *The Alien Sky*, but by reintroducing it in *The Quartet*, he has added a new dimension to the epic drama of the Raj's collapse.

Susan's bridegroom, Captain Bingham, had at first shown attention to Sarah and not to Susan. Teddy and Susan surprised everyone by their wedding announcement. Teddy was of course a most eligible bachelor, "Pukka," handsome, and a Muzzy Guide. He is posted to Mirat so the wedding has to be there. The Nawab has put everything at their disposal and even designated Ahmed Kasim to help them with all their needs. Because Teddy's friend Tony Bishop falls ill at the last minute and cannot be best man, Teddy asks the man with whom he shares his quarters who happens to be Ronald Merrick. Merrick agrees and is present at the wedding through "chance alone" (S, 173).

But the wedding is marred by three incidents, two of which are echoes of the Bibighar affair. First, there is the incident of the stone. A stone is hurled at the black limousine, a 1926 Daimler, with the prominent crest of the Nawab on its door, carrying Merrick and Teddy on their way to the wedding. The glass is shattered, and Teddy gets a cut below his cheekbone. The second incident occurs at the Club. The Nawab of Mirat, an honored guest at the wedding, is refused entry into the Gymkhana Club by two M.P.'s because he is an Indian. But the error is rectified and dignity restored.

The third incident concerns an Indian woman in a white saree. This occurs on the platform of the Mirat train station as Susan and Teddy are ready to go to Nanoora for their honeymoon. The Indian woman in the white saree appears from nowhere, and falls at Merrick's feet and appeals to him in Hindi to help her. Merrick is embarrassed, as are other members of the wedding party, and a railway official pulls the woman away. We learn later when Merrick and Sarah meet and talk that the woman in the white saree was Kumar's aunt, and that Pandit Baba had put her up to create this awkward scene. The stone and the appearance of the Indian woman both make their points. The Bibighar affair has not been forgotten. Merrick is a marked man.

Bronowski meets Merrick after the wedding and deftly steers the conversation to the Bibighar affair. This provides an opportunity for Merrick to give his version of the Bibighar affair. He is firmly convinced that Kumar is the culprit.

Now that we have Merrick's version of the Bibighar affair, there remains Kumar's version. It is one of the most forceful and dramatic sections of *The Scorpion* and of *The Quartet* as a whole. It is a novel within a novel and can stand by itself.

We have learned that Kumar is in Kandipat jail serving sentence not for the rape for which he was suspected (and on which Merrick is firm) but on the flimsy charge of having known Motilal, a political activist. Kumar could have languished in prison completely forgotten, but because of Lady Manners's interest in the case Kumar receives a private hearing, in May, 1944, "One year, nine months and twelve days later" (*S*, 273).

Accompanied by Captain Nigel Robert Alexander Rowan, a product of Chillingborough like Kumar, his excellency the governor's personal choice for the task, Lady Manners arrives at the Kandipat jail. Taking her seat in an austere room she becomes the invisible audience to the hearing that is to be conducted. She has a private line of communication with Captain Rowan who, together with an Indian official from the Home and Law Department, Mr. Vallabhai Ramaswamy Gopal, and an Indian clerk, constitute the hearing committee.

The scene is set in such a manner that although we are familiar with the charges against Kumar, and have by now heard Daphne's version, Merrick's version, and the official versions of Brigadier Reid and Robin White, we are eager to hear what Kumar has to say. The dialogue, cast in the form of courtroom proceedings, is alive and realistic and lends itself for a tense, dramatic stage play.

Kumar enters hesitantly. He is a modern-day Philoctetes and writes under that pseudonym in the fourth and concluding volume, *A Division of the Spoils*. The hearing in Kandipat Jail gives us a frightening look into the depths of his tortured and alienated psyche. He wants nothing more than to go home, home being England. But

England does not want this brown Englishman. His own family because of his travel abroad makes him drink cow urine to purify him. To Englishmen in India including his friend, Colin, he is invisible. To Indians he is a "lickspittle of the Raj." He finds himself trapped in this prison of infinite barriers. He turns to Daphne, an English girl, but their love is doomed from the beginning, for he is a son of the subject race and she is a daughter of the Raj, and men like Merrick with their own tortured versions of the mystique of the Empire, are self-appointed vigilantes prowling in an alien land to break up such a union of heart and mind.

At the end of this hearing Kumar emerges as a tragic figure, "an English boy with a dark brown skin, a hopeless combination" (S, 269), a permanent indictment of the British rule in India, "the left-over loose end."

Kumar keeps his promise to Daphne by repeating that he had not met her that fateful night. When he hears of the death of Daphne he weeps silently and regrets answering all these questions. Kumar tells of Merrick's relentless questioning and sadistic physical torture and the perverted pleasure he derived by fondling his private parts. Just by being an Indian, even before anything had taken place, he had in the eyes of Merrick become the guilty party.

To Lady Manners who is convinced that Kumar is telling the truth, it is all a charade. "Nothing can happen to Merrick, can it?—everything in the file is the uncorroborated evidence of the prisoner. Nothing will touch him. That is part of the charade, too" (S, 307), she observes.

Kumar will be released, Rowan assures her. This is the last time we see him. In the following two volumes we only hear about him.

The story shifts from the Kandipat jail to Pankot, and British reverses in Burma, Imphal, and Kohima bringing the Japanese onto Indian soil. This development sends tremors of anxiety through the British community in Pankot. The tragedy of the war is brought even closer when Teddy Bingham, husband of Susan, is killed on the Burma front. Susan is pregnant with his child.

Teddy's death pushes Susan dangerously into a world of her own. Her melancholy becomes a topic of conversation among the Pankot Memsahibs as they gather for tea and bridge.

The entire Anglo-Indian community in Pankot rallies to support and sympathize with Susan and the Laytons. Letters of sympathy pour in from friends and contacts. One such letter informs the Laytons that when Teddy was killed, Ronald Merrick had been with him; that Merrick himself was wounded in the skirmish that took Teddy's life and that he was recuperating in an army base hospital. Sarah thinks of writing to him but they hear from Merrick. Reading it the impression is left that Merrick is seriously wounded, probably lost his eyes, his limbs. Sarah decides to visit him in Calcutta where he has been transferred.

Propped up by pillows and dressed in "a complex of bandage and gauze around his head," as a result of third degree burns and facing the prospect of his left arm being completely amputated, Merrick greets Sarah. He tells her the reason for Teddy's death. In the manner of Teddy's death the theme of the disappearance of the Raj is reinforced.

Teddy had been deeply disturbed by the development of Jiffs, Indian soldiers who were Japanese POW's turning coat and ending up as collaborators with the Japanese. Teddy found it difficult to believe that "Indian soldiers who've eaten the king's salt and been proud to serve in the army generation after generation could be suborned like that" (*S*, 374). Capturing Jiffs and pumping them for information was Merrick's special job. Teddy had become overly concerned with this question, fearful that one of the Jiffs might turn out to be a Muzzy Guide (Muzzafir Guide). Teddy firmly believed in the regimental mystique, had conviction that he was still father and mother—*Man-bap*—to his men.

It was in connection with the capture of a Jiff and Teddy's attempt to make the man realize his mistake that Teddy got killed. The captured Indian soldier had responded to Teddy's I-am-still-your-Father-and-Mother formula, and had "knelt down and put his head on Teddy's boots" (*S*, 387), which of course had profoundly moved Teddy. The soldier had given Teddy names of two other Indian soldiers, both Jiffs, both Muzzy Guides, and Teddy had gone out to find them and do his *Man-bap* formula on them. In the attempt he was burned badly by an explosion and had died. As Merrick recollects the fire that burned Teddy to death, he remembers Edwina Crane's self-immolation, and her picture of the jewel in her crown. That picture allegorically presented the essence of the *Man-bap*, as Indians dutifully gathered around Queen Victoria, looking upon her as mother and father. Crane had killed herself because she no longer had faith in the *Man-bap* ideal of her country. Teddy got killed because he could not accept the death of the *Man-bap* ideal. By implying the contrast between Crane's death and Teddy's the link is once again established between *The Jewel* and *The Scorpion*.

Sarah leaves Merrick with an uneasy feeling, for Merrick to her is "our dark side, the arcane side. You reveal something that is sad about us, as if out here we had built a mansion without doors and windows, with no way in and no way out" (*S*, 398). When her Aunt Fenny tries to be a matchmaker between Merrick and her, Sarah says that Merrick, "appalls" her (*S*, 407).

Later that night Sarah goes out with a Major Clark, another Chillingburian like Kumar, Rowan, and her own father. After a stop at the Grand Hotel and a visit to an Indian house where there is a party in progress, Major Clark somewhat unceremoniously seduces the virgin Sarah in a back room.

On a brief stopover in Ranpur to change trains to Pankot she runs into Count Bronowski, and Captain Rowan is travelling with him.

By the time Sarah reaches Pankot her aunt Mabel is dead. Susan, alone at that time, watches Mabel's death and goes into shock and premature labor, and thirty-three hours later gives birth to a boy who looks "absurdly, touchingly, like Teddy" (*S*, 478).

Mabel Layton is buried in St. John's in Pankot. This shocks Barbara Batchelor, the loyal friend of Mabel. Barbie insists that Mabel's last wish was to be buried in St. Luke's in Ranpur next to her husband. But Mildred, who has all along both despised and hated Barbie, turns a deaf ear. The tensions caused by this burial and a more elaborate portrait of Barbie appears in the following volume of *The Quartet*, *The Towers of Silence*.

Susan's melancholy intensifies to the point of madness. One evening Susan dresses young Teddy, lays him on the grass in front of Rose Cottage, sprinkles a wide circle of kerosene around him, and sets fire to it. Minnie, the child's nurse, observing this, manages to rescue the child.

The Scorpion concludes with Susan in a nursing home under heavy guard and protection.

III   The Towers of Silence

In *The Towers of Silence*, the third volume of *The Quartet*, the world of the sahibs and memsahibs, intricate and hierarchical, is microscopically examined. We have had a nodding acquaintance with Lucy Smalley in *The Scorpion*. Her husband joins her in this volume and they wait, as it were, to come into their own in Scott's last novel, *Staying On*. Merrick's servant, Suleiman, the Pathan[8] who becomes more noticeable in the concluding volume, makes a brief appearance in *The Towers*.

In this volume, the novelist goes backward to 1939, the farthest he has gone in *The Quartet*, to move forward to 1945, the period covered.

Some of the characters from the previous two volumes reappear: all the four Layton women; Ronald Merrick; Teddy Bingham, whose wedding and death we have witnessed; and Barbara Batchelor. We get to know them more as they reveal themselves with all their subtler nuances of feelings and opinions.

New characters are introduced, particularly members of the Anglo-Indian community in Pankot and Ranpur. With the use of letters and newspaper reports, the novelist brings the central theme of *The Quartet*, the Bibighar affair, back into the picture. New versions of the affair are presented and examined, particularly by members of the Anglo-Indian community in Pankot. The defection of the Indian soldiers from the British Indian army to the INA which was a murmur in *The Scorpion* becomes a deafening roar in *The Towers*.

There are three exceptional women characters in *The Towers*. We have had a casual acquaintance with all three of them in *The Scorpion*, but in *The Towers* they receive the full treatment and emerge as complex and fascinating portraits of the Raj women.

There is Mabel Layton, the tough elderly widow of James Layton, the mistress of Rose Cottage, a recluse, who has withdrawn into her rose garden but who knows it is not possible for a Britisher to be a recluse in India because "even when the British are alone, they are on show, representing something" (*T*, 23).

Then there is Mildred Layton, wife of Colonel Layton and daughter-in-law of Mabel, the last of the memsahibs, "made of stone, splendidly upright" (*T*, 256), playing out her role in the absence of her husband, a POW in Europe, and putting on the stern facade: all was well with the Raj.

Then of course there is Barbara (Barbie for short) Batchelor, the retired Protestant missionary school teacher from Ranpur. It is through Barbie's eyes that most of the events in *The Towers* are seen. She is one of the key figures. It is also Barbie lying ill in bed, in the hospital in Ranpur, who watches the towers of silence, the place where the Parsees leave their dead for the vultures. The hovering vultures waiting to pick the dead bodies clean symbolize to her the carcass of the British Raj waiting to be picked clean.

The volume begins with Barbie's retirement from her post as superintendent of the Protestant Mission Schools in Ranpur. A devout Christian, she is evangelical in spirit and believes that teaching children the word of God is more important than teaching them about the world. She is the opposite of Edwina Crane who did not give a hoot about Bible lessons, and whom Barbie had succeeded in Muzzafirabad. Barbie knew Mr. Cleghorn who had given the portrait of the jewel in her crown to Crane and had told Barbie how Crane had often used that picture to teach her class. Barbie has a copy of the picture.

When Barbie retired she had no plans and no place to go. She responds to an advertisement in *The Ranpur Gazette* by Mabel Layton asking for a single woman to share accommodations with her at Rose Cottage in Pankot. She promptly receives a favorable reply from Mabel and leaves for Pankot with her trunkful of personal belongings and is met by Mabel's old servant, Aziz.

In spite of their odd and conflicting modes of behavior—Barbie's passion for nonstop talking and Mabel's passion for silence—they hit it off. Mabel expansively tells Barbie to be completely at home and Barbie soon works herself into the role of a co-hostess. Such a takeover of duties brings her into confrontation with Mildred Layton who feels her position usurped by Barbie.

A curious and interesting relationship develops between Mabel and Barbie. As the novel progresses Barbie develops a protective and passionate friendship and loyalty to Mabel. This loyalty alienates her from Mildred who misses no opportunity to insult Barbie. She is deliberately not invited to Susan's wedding reception, an event to which Barbie had looked forward.

Mabel is detached and indifferent to this conflict. Mildred's compulsive and systematic drinking increases and so do her unpaid bills. It is Sarah who restores a semblance of order and tranquillity between the warring factions in the household, helpfully settling her mother's bills "before they became an embarrassment" (*T*, 37). It is also Sarah who is much more communicative with her aunt Mabel and patient with Barbie's chatter. Barbie, of course, thinks the world of Sarah and is concerned for her because if Sarah is "not careful she'll find herself not living, just helping others to" (*T*, 168). Sarah's consideration and courtesy to Barbie acts as an irritant to her mother, and we see the beginnings of the later hostility by her toward Sarah.

The tensions and conflicts between the women at Rose Cottage from trivia to major issues is carefully and realistically presented.

Barbie is as prodigious a letter writer as she is a nonstop chatterer. When she reads in *The Ranpur Gazette* a feature story under the title "English Woman Attacked" involving her friend and "heroine" Edwina Crane, Barbie begins to write one of her several lengthy letters to Crane. None of these are answered. But the news story and Barbie's letters bring the attack on Crane and the Bibighar affair back into the picture. The letters also reveal the various versions of the affair as Barbie had heard them from a variety of Mayapore visitors coming into Pankot, and the reactions of the Anglo-Indian community to these reports.

Thus the events of the past are brought to attention, its reverberations noted.

Crane's death makes Barbie long for an apotheosis of her own, "nothing spectacular, mind, nothing in the least grandiose nor even just grand but, like Edwina's, quiet with a still-centre to it" (*T*, 65). She sees in the image of the unknown Indian whose dead hand Crane had held, a metaphor of what her own life in India had been: unknown!

The novel moves on to give us a more detailed picture of Edward Arthur David Bingham—"Teddy." We have read about his ill-fated wedding in Mirat in *The Scorpion*. In *The Towers* we read about his honeymoon in Nanoora the hill station.

In filling us in on parts of Teddy's life left out in *The Scorpion*, Merrick is reintroduced. In briefing Teddy's army unit on the INA and Indian soldiers defecting to it, we get an exhaustive account of the origins and development of this new force that posed a serious threat to the mystique of the Empire. This army of New India, *Azad Hind Fauz*, had its birth both in Tokyo and Berlin by Subhas Chandra Bose. It was an army that would march "alongside the Japanese not as traitors and stooges but as patriots and men of destiny" (*T*, 128). They planned their entry onto Indian soil and believed that the Indian soldiers would join them, that the Indian people would support them, and they would begin their triumphant march on Delhi. Merrick is brutally realistic in his assessment of the INA. He does not minimize the psychological impact of this traumatic turn of events. In this he reveals himself to be a shrewd intelligence officer.

But Teddy finds it hard to accept the hard fact of "King's Commissioned Officers leading their men—our own men—against" (*T*, 147), the British. He fervently believes that this turn of events will change and that "ninety percent of the people who've joined the INA" (*T*, 146), would return at the first opportunity. It is this conviction as we have noted in *The Scorpion* that leads to his death.

Outside Teddy's and Merrick's quarters a bicycle and chalk marks of a cabalistic design appear. Merrick is being pursued. The bicycle in *The Towers*, the stone that hits the limousine in Mirat, and the Indian woman in the white saree on the platform of the Mirat train station in *The Scorpion* are all reminders that Merrick's role in the Bibighar affair has not and will not be forgotten.

In *The Scorpion* we read about Mabel Layton's death, in *The Towers* we get a more detailed version of that death and its shattering impact on Barbie.

Several weeks prior to her death, Mabel had made a casual comment that she would never go to Ranpur again, "at least not until I'm buried" (*T*, 183). This casual comment of Mabel becomes a command to Barbie, with all the sanctity of a last will and testament, her dear friend's sacred wish that she be buried in Ranpur.

Barbie is at the house of Edgar Maybrick, a widower and a retired tea planter, when she learns of her friend's death. She wants to rush right back to Rose Cottage, but the Peplows, the clergyman and his wife, dissuade Barbie from leaving to prevent a scene between her and Mildred Layton. Barbie senses a plot on the part of the Peplows to keep her with them while a hasty burial of Mabel takes place. She escapes and walks all the way back to Rose Cottage. There she becomes even more distraught listening to Mildred cast suspicion on Aziz, Mabel's old and loyal servant, who is missing.

With grim determination Barbie is set to carry out her friend's desires. She goes to the hospital where Mabel's body has been taken and learns to her dismay that arrangements have been made by Mildred for Mabel's burial in Pankot in St. John's. Nothing can stop Barbie now, the duty born out of loyalty to Mabel, her one and only friend, takes on a messianic religious significance, her apotheosis as it were. She forces her way into the mortuary to identify her friend's body and possibly remove it for the proper burial. After her first glimpse of "an authentic vision of hell" (*T*, 230), she is ushered out.

Her next move is to confront Mildred who has taken a room at the hospital to await the birth of Susan's baby, her first grandchild. But when Barbie knocks on her door, Mildred who is really awaiting the arrival of her lover, Captain Kevin Coley, is embarrassed to see Barbie and is adamant and sarcastic to Barbie's appeal.

Mabel is buried in Pankot and Barbie sees in it, "an act of callousness: the sin of collectively not caring a damn about a desire or an expectation of the fulfillment of a promise" (*T*, 236). This lack of care and concern, symbolizes to Barbie the tragedy of the Raj itself in India.

Aziz returns, and is silent about his absence, refusing to explain it, implying that he had his own rights and private reason to mourn the way he wants to for his memsahib Mabel. Barbie alone understands him, and in their brief exchanges there is "an undertone of parable" (*T*, 258).

With Mabel gone, Barbie has no place to go. Aziz can at least go to his people in the hills, but Barbie with her belongings, particularly her trunk containing "her history," is at a loss. And according to Emerson, Barbie's favorite author, without one's history, one is not explained (*T*, 263). The Peplows offer her temporary shelter.

At the Peplows, Barbie is not happy, for Clarissa Peplow has no place for Barbie's belongings. Clarissa is also nervous about Barbie because of the rumor she has heard that Barbie could be a lesbian and hence had been asked by Mildred to leave Rose Cottage. The accusation shocks Barbie and gives her a glimpse of Mildred's enormous hatred for her.

It is Sarah who extends her compassion for Barbie and offers to keep Barbie's trunk with her. But Barbie decides to leave it with the Mali in his shed in a corner.

Even away from Rose Cottage Barbie feels the hostility of Mildred's anger, for Mildred is strongly convinced that Barbie is evil and that it was her presence which had brought bad luck to Susan. Mildred returns the twelve silver apostle spoons, Barbie's gift to Susan, through Clarissa Peplow. To Barbie this is the final insult, but she decides to give the spoons as a gift to the officers mess in Pankot, through Captain Kevin Coley, Mildred's lover. But when she goes to call on him she blunders into seeing Coley and Mildred in lustful intercourse "active in a human parody of divine creation" (*T*, 300). The sight shocks her, and she rushes out and walks back dazed in pouring rain to the Peplows. This results in bronchial pneumonia and she is hospitalized.

By the time she recovers, Rose Cottage is to be closed and Barbie goes to Rose Cottage to remove her trunk. There she runs into Captain Merrick who has just arrived from Calcutta to call on the Laytons. But the Laytons have gone to Calcutta to stay with Arthur Grace, Sarah's uncle.

Merrick remembers Barbie from a conversation he once had had with Edwina Crane, and talk about Crane leads inevitably to talk about the Bibighar affair. Merrick is obsessed with this affair, ever ready to talk about it to anyone who is prepared to listen. He milks every opportunity to restate his case, reconfirm his belief that he was right. He cannot get either Kumar or Daphne out of his system. It is a new trait we notice in Merrick, this passionate obsession.

Merrick helps Barbie with her trunk, and Barbie gives him her copy of the jewel in her crown. Merrick is the proper person to have it, for he alone still believes in the mystique of the Empire and *Man-bap*. But as the two of them ride in a tonga with the trunk there is an explosion and the horse panics. She is hurt and her trunk falls and breaks open scattering her "history."

Images of past, present, and future crowd in upon Barbie as she lies sick in the hospital. Her delirious mind sees birds and butterflies flutter and rest in her hair. The passages describing Barbie's last few days as she is snarled up in the cobwebs of memory and melancholy are both poetic and tragic in their intensity. Her insights into British decay are illuminated with bursts of truth as she catches the vultures through her window.

With a brief excerpt from a letter by MAK to Mahatma Gandhi which notes the election of the socialist government in London, and the dropping of the atomic bomb over Hiroshima, and wondering which one of the two would have the greater impact on India's future, the third volume of *The Quartet, The Towers*, comes to a conclusion.

IV   A Division of the Spoils

The final volume of *The Quartet*, which took longer to write than the other three volumes, covers the years between 1945 and 1947. The first half of the volume concerns itself with events between 1945 and 1946, while the second half is completely devoted to 1947, the year of the Raj's departure. All the themes, stories, and characters from the previous three volumes reappear, or are referred to, repeated, and remembered and seen from different points of view.

In *A Division* the imperial embrace of the two nations, India and Britain, is broken. The voices of those, both Indian such as MAK, and British such as Lady Manners, who cry "only connect"—to borrow a Forsterian expression—is drowned out by the chorus of "only separate," and division is the result.

Newspaper reports, editorials, extracts from diaries, journal entries, a series of political cartoons, dialogues in the best dramatic and dialectical sense, monologues of a stream-of-consciousness nature, are all made use of, to orchestrate the multifaceted and multilayered themes, and the wide and extraordinary range of characters to describe the intricate complexities of the final negotiations for British departure.

Of all the volumes in *The Quartet, A Division* is the most complex, for "Paul Scott makes nothing simple; thus his work bears a disturbing resemblance to life" and he "makes few concessions to the reader."⁹ More than in any other work of his, "Scott reveals in *A Division* his refusal to compromise with those who would wish to hurry the story along."¹⁰

For the most part events are seen by Sergeant Guy Perceval Lancelot Perron, a new character introduced in *A Division*, to draw all the various strands of the story together and provide through his journal a commentary, like a Greek chorus, on the crumbling and departing carcass of the British Raj.

Perron, Cambridge educated, a tough, detached intellectual with an interest in Indian history, specially from "Eighteen-thirty to the Mutiny" (*D*, 88), because it is during this period that the "dress rehearsal for full imperial rule" (*D*, 88) took place, is in many ways Scott's alter ego. Scott paints himself into the picture in this last volume, and the physical description of Perron could very adequately describe Scott himself, "nearly six feet tall and with shoulders like an ox" (*D*, 174). Like Perron, Scott too was in army intelligence during his stint of service in India.

Perron is in India operating under the cover of AEC (Army Education Corps) to investigate Indian independence movements.

If one character is to be selected as presiding over *A Division*, it is Merrick, who is also deep in military intelligence questioning returning Indians from INA. Merrick is still enigmatic, still touching everybody with his activities, with defects and virtues too close to be separated.

The war in Europe is over and peace is a month old. The atomic bomb has brought Japan to its knees and the British in India are involved in the difficult negotiations of the transfer of power. It is no longer a question of are we leaving? It is a question of how, and to whom, should power be transferred. Thus as Perron notes, the British were rationalizing the dissolution of this Empire for "moral reasons" (*D*, 106).

Paul Scott uses a series of political cartoons by "Halki," an Indian cartoonist, to present the complexities of these negotiations with parties and personalities involved in the break up of "the imperial embrace." Later on in *A Division*, the transfer of power is seen from the point of view of the princely State of Mirat. We became familiar with Mirat, a mere yellow speck of a state which the British had let flourish, when we attended Susan and Teddy's wedding in *The Scorpion*. Hindus and Muslims, Princes and Anglo-Indians, all wait for the inevitable changes that will come with the departure of the Raj. Mirat becomes a microcosm of the rest of India. It is against this background that the major and minor characters of *A Division* act out their final roles. The volume opens with an evening at the Maharanee's in Bombay where "officers and men fraternize, not to mention white, black and in between" (*D*, 20). Perron attends the party because he hopes to pick up bits of intelligence about any possible attempt by members of any popular movement to liberate soldiers and officials of the INA who are in prison awaiting trial. "The whole thing's an utter waste of time" (*D*, 21), according to a Major Purvis, who is the one who brings the party to Perron's attention.

To the party also comes "an English girl; but not just an English girl, *the* English girl" (*D*, 39), Sarah Layton. She has been in Bombay to welcome her father Colonel James Layton, returned from Europe after his grim experiences as a German POW. She is to escort him home to Ranpur, and he is waiting for some Indian soldiers from the Pankot regiment who are recovering in a hospital, before they could all journey together.

Also present at the party is Ronald Merrick with his burned left face and his artificial hand hidden beneath a glove, also in intelligence and also for the purpose of picking up information concerning INA and its soldiers. Merrick is interested in questioning these men and finding out *why* they joined the INA.

Perron speaks fluent Urdu and Merrick, his superior in rank, has used Perron's linguistic ability to interrogate an Indian soldier named Karim Muzzafir Khan who had joined the German-based branch of the INA—*Frei-Hind*.

Hari Kumar has already popped up in their conversation, Chillingborough being the point of contact, for Perron too is a product of Chillingborough. All that Perron remembers of Kumar at Chillingborough is Kumar's fondness for cricket and his ignorance about the difference between *karma* and *dharma*, Indian philosophic concepts.

Also at the party is Ahmed Kasim, who is accompanying Count Bronowski. The Count immediately questions Perron endlessly about his background and reason for being in India.

The Maharanee, who prefers to be called Aimee, ex-wife of the Maharajah of Kotala, is an eccentric odd ball. She can either throw a party that lasts for a day or two or terminate it within an hour after it begins. There are curly-haired blond British sailors with wealthy but lonely and aging tea planters; British airmen in sarees; a beefy looking

American officer who makes a pass at Perron, and Aneila, "a young Indian girl of gazelle-like charm" (*D*, 34), the Maharanee's niece. The liquor flows, the atmosphere grows languid with hints and promises of orgies and Bacchanalian revelry. It is all a bit too much for self-righteous Merrick, who calls the colorful gathering "scum," and decides to leave with Sarah.

The party breaks up because the Maharanee wants it to. Perron stops in briefly to report to Major Purvis who had directed him to the party, but finds Purvis passed out in an attempted suicide. After rescuing him, Perron is invited by Merrick to join him in the Laytons' apartment which is in the same building. Here Perron meets Sarah's father, Colonel Layton.

Colonel Layton is anxious to meet his family in Ranpur, but even more anxious to meet an Indian soldier from his own regiment in Delhi. The son of a man who had won the Victoria Cross, he is the only Indian from Pankot regiment who had joined the *Frei-Hind* movement in Germany. This defection has shaken Colonel Layton, in much the same way it had disturbed and caused the death of his son-in-law, Teddy.

The train journey from Bombay to Ranpur, taking Sarah and her father in one compartment, and the Indian soldiers in another, is beautifully described. The feelings of returning home after a long period, the subtleties and complexities of overcoming uneasiness in covering those distances between people who are closely related, is subtly and touchingly integrated into the train journey. Layton has not only traveled long distances geographically, but has to travel emotional and psychological distances as well.

Pankot is reached. The rose gardens that Mabel had once tended so carefully have been cemented over for tennis courts. Even the name Rose Cottage is now just a prosaic address, Upper Club Road. Reunion takes place between Colonel Layton, his daughter, Susan, wife Mildred, and grandson, Teddy, Jr. Sarah withdraws to let them all experience the homecoming and reunion by themselves.

Sarah learns of Barbie's death and calls up the mother superior at the hospital where she had died and learns through a somewhat bad telephone connection that Barbie has left some things for her. Sarah writes to Nigel Rowan who is now chief aide to Governor Malcolm asking his help to get in touch with the hospital and find out what it is she has to do. Sarah's letter acts as a catalyst, and Nigel recollects, relaxing in a bath tub, "their first meeting, just over a year ago" (*D*, 146). This "recollection" of Rowan gives us Rowan's perspective on the Bibighar affair from a knowledge of official documents he was privy to.

Thoughts of his past meeting stirs his fondness for Sarah, and he calls her, ostensibly to tell her that he followed up on her letter and has picked up a small package left by Barbie for her, but in reality to reestablish contact with her again. Merrick creeps into their telephone conversation and before long Rowan meets the man himself.

The encounter takes place in the train station in Ranpur; Merrick is on his way to Pankot with his servant and personal bodyguard and spy, Suleiman, the pathan. This "bazaar pathan; handsome, predatory" (*D*, 200), clean shaven but pock marked, his eyes rimmed with Kohl is "instinctively distrusted" (*D*, 200) by Rowan. Merrick personally wants to interrogate the Havildar who had joined the *Frei-Hind* in Germany. But the Havildar is dead, having hung himself because Merrick had shamed and insulted him. A coffin with his dead body is on the train with Merrick. The only reason for Merrick making this trip is "to sustain the connection" with the Laytons in Pankot.

Perron, who is traveling with Merrick because Merrick is his superior, is bothered and irritated by him. Perron is particularly contemptuous of Suleiman whom he nicknames "the Red Shadow." But the prospect of seeing Sarah makes "several days in Pankot bearable" to Perron (*D*, 212).

When they arrive in Pankot, Perron finds some comic relief in one of the British NCO's in the General Hospital, a Corporal Dixon, "known affectionately as Sophie, or Miss Dixon, or Mum" (*D*, 225). With his high camp humor and broad humanism, Dixon is a safety valve who tells scurrilous but funny stories . . . "in a tone of prim outrage, of astonishment at the trickery and underhandedness of the world" (*D*, 226). Dixon promptly baptizes Suleiman the Pathan as "Miss Khyber Pass, 1935," and Merrick as "Dracula."

In Pankot Merrick has set up an elaborate stage show for his recording of statements from ex-POW's. But the whole show is pointless because the man to be questioned is dead and, as Perron observes, "the little *mise en scene* was a vivid example of the extraordinary care Merrick took to manipulate things, people and objects into some kind of significant objective/subjective order with himself at the dominating and controlling centre" (*D*, 230).

After the "show" in Pankot Merrick departs for further work on INA men in Singapore and leaves his Pathan servant with Perron to help him. But the Pathan turns out to be both a pickpocket and a spy for Merrick so Perron boots him out with the help of Potter, an NCO. Potter tells Perron of a dirty trick Merrick had played on an NCO called "Pinky."

A harmless, friendly, intelligent, and conscientious individual, Pinky had worked in base hospitals and was working as a clerk in the office of psychiatrist Richardson, when Merrick had chosen him as his victim. Pinky had access to all the confidential files on men under treatment. Pinky, who was a homosexual, had discovered while looking through the files that quite a few of them had confessed to the doctor that they had "mucked about" with other guys, that it "just happened quite naturally" (*D*, 249). None of these soldiers had been discharged but rather recommended as fit for active duty. Pinky's earlier guilt about his homosexuality began to fade. Merrick enlists his Pathan to exploit Pinky's sexual preferences to trap him into an embarrassing situation. With the fear of blackmail hanging over him, Pinky gives Merrick the key to the private files of patients under Dr. Richardson's care. Merrick, who has plans to marry Susan, is interested in finding out about her as she is under Richardson's care. Merrick uses this devious way to check up on her, and in the process walks all over Pinky.

Accompanied by Rowan, Perron calls on the Laytons for dinner. Later, when Rowan and Perron converse and reminisce about Chillingborough—which they had both attended—Colin Lindsey's name comes up. If Colin is talked about can Kumar be far behind? Thus Kumar is reintroduced, and Perron's curiosity about him makes Rowan tell Perron of his role in Kumar's case during the hearing in the Kandipat jail.

According to Rowan, it is Colin's rejection of Kumar that brought Kumar and Merrick to confront each other and inaugurated the tragedy that seems to have no end. Yet it had been a logical meeting, between "Kumar—one of Macaulay's brown skinned Englishmen— and Merrick, English born and English bred, but a man whose country's social and economic structure had denied him advantages and privileges which Kumar had initially enjoyed" (*D*, 301).

Through Rowan we learn of Kumar's life after his release; the help offered by Gopal in trying to get him some students to teach English; and Rowan's correspondence with Kumar. He gives Perron Kumar's address because he wants to track down Kumar. His curiosity increases when Perron reads a feature story titled "Alma Mater" in the *Ranpur Gazette* by Philoctetes. It is the last paragraph in this piece that touches Perron, a passage full of nostalgia for England, full of the sadness of exile. Perron identifies Philoctetes as Kumar, an ideal pseudonym that Kumar has selected, for he too, is permanently banished because of his own kind of smell.

In a following monologue we get Sarah's thinking, her putting all the pieces of her life together to get some sense out of it, and her desire to go home to England to stay with one of her aunts. In a father and daughter conversation, Sarah expresses her concern that Susan in her state is "not fit to marry anyone let alone Merrick" (*D*, 367). When her father sees a lot of admirable qualities in Merrick, even "moral courage," Sarah retorts, "I'd prefer to see some moral cowardice or whatever it makes you admit that there can be two sides to a question, other points of view as good as your own" (*D*, 366).

Merrick, who has been promoted to lieutenant colonel, meets with MAK to brief him on the charges against his elder sons, Sayed's, role in the INA, before he takes him to Delhi for the INA trials.

Father and son, MAK and Sayed meet. In their meeting and their opposing viewpoints, Sayed opting for Pakistan and MAK firm on a united India; Sayed breaking a contract to join the INA and MAK meticulously arguing with his legal skill the futility of Sayed's action; Sayed's emotional rhetoric and MAK's cool logic, the sharp divisions within one family as a result of the impending division of India is dramatically presented.

The second part of *A Division* begins with an analysis of a series of political cartoons by Halki to inform and reflect the various stages involved in the transfer of power. Perron, who admires Halki, has been in England and has returned to India for "academic reasons"; he is "primarily concerned with the relationship between the Crown and the Indian States" (*D*, 473). The future of the nearly six hundred princely states is of course irrevocably tied up with either India or Pakistan. But some Englishmen, who desperately hope that some of the states can carve out their independence separately from either India or Pakistan, are attempting to work out a personal contract as advisors to these states. Sir Robert Conway (from *Birds of Paradise*) is one, Rowan is another, and so is Merrick, who is already in Mirat at the invitation of Bronowski to reorganize the Mirat police.

Perron visits Mirat where he has been invited, because he wants to watch from a ringside seat the fate of the princely states, when the Raj on whom they had so confidently depended departs. In Mirat Perron learns from the *Mirat Courier* of Merrick's death—"as a result of injuries sustained in a riding accident" (*D*, 486)—and funeral services.

Merrick, however, has died a more violent death. Perron's curiosity in wanting to know the last days of Merrick and the manner in which Merrick died is again a novel within a novel. When the Raj departed Merrick had not wanted to return to England. He had wanted to stay on, if not in India maybe in Pakistan, possibly in the old rugged Northwest Frontier Provinces, the home of the Pathans, where administering justice was not always by the book.

But Merrick was murdered, dressed in the Pathan outfit he used to wear when he went out with other Pathans to spy on people. He had been "hacked to pieces with his own ornamental axe and strangled with his own sash" (*D*, 548), and one of his murderers had scrawled the word Bibighar on Susan's dressing-table mirror.

His murderers were never found, for the operation had been carefully planned. Bronowski has the proper epitaph for Merrick when he says, "he sought the occasion of his own death and that he grew impatient for it . . . he wanted what happened to happen. Perhaps he hoped that his murder would be avenged in some splendidly spectacular way, in a kind of Wagnerian climax, the *Raj* emerging from the twilight and sweeping down from the hills with flaming swords" (*D*, 571).

Young Teddy Bingham, to whom Merrick was really daddy, has the picture the jewel in her crown; the picture Merrick had received from Barbie; the picture that Crane had received from Mr. Cleghorn as a gift; the picture that opened *The Quartet*.

Mirat acceeds to India and becomes the scene of both celebrations and riots. Violence flares up between the Hindus and Muslims but the English are suddenly universally popular.

The exodus from Mirat begins. The Muslims want to get out and the Hindus want to get in, with the English families scrambling to get on the last train out of Mirat. What was taking place in Mirat was happening all over the greater part of the subcontinent. This mass movement, the largest ever in human civilization, is dramatized with total impact in this "yellow speck" of a state, Mirat, and in the fate of one man, on one train, from Mirat bound to Ranpur. The crowded train with Hindus, Muslims, and the English has to pass through an area lined with fanatics. Perron, Sarah, Susan, and Ahmed are among others on this train.

Half an hour later the train is stopped and attacked but none of the English are touched. The apolitical Ahmed Kasim, with a smile, offers himself so that the train can continue with the others. "It seems to be me they want" he says and steps out. No one goes out to help him. He is hacked to pieces.

In dramatizing the death of one individual the tragic impact of the division is conveyed sharply.

The novel concludes with Perron on the trail of Kumar, walking the narrow streets "where no Englishman had ever walked before" (*D*, 546) in the slums of Ranpur. But Kumar is not in his house. It was just as well, for there was not much Perron could have said to him, to the boy whom he had once asked what *karma* and *dharma* meant. Kumar was living it.

CHAPTER 7

The Raj Quartet *as History*

P AUL Scott described *The Quartet* as a "sequence of four novels about the closing years of British rule in India. The characters were imaginary. So were the events. The framework was as historically accurate as I could make it."[1]

To obtain this historical accuracy, Scott immersed himself for over twenty-five years in the study of Indian history; consulted and checked facts with experts in the India office of the British Museum; made three trips to the subcontinent where he traveled extensively to get the feel and tempo of his locales; and took ten years to complete the novel sequence. He therefore brings to his major achievement a remarkable combination of a historian's meticulous concern for documentation and factual truth, and the novelist's concern for aesthetic truth. The result is a stunning portrait of a people and a place no formal history can give. Scott knows his facts and makes them come alive as he explores human nature under stress in a period of violent and traumatic change. The historical framework and his vivid characterizations give us a staggering sense of total participation.

Scott did not wish to be categorized as a historical novelist of the period 1942–1947, the time span covered by *The Quartet*. He was right in this insistence, for *The Quartet* is by no means a sequence of historical novels in the confining definition of an historical novel. He was a modern novelist deeply interested in the society in which he lived. He chose India as an extended metaphor for his personal view of life, and offered an explanation for such a choice. "The India in the novels I write about India is used as a metaphor for mine. If I write about Anglo-India in 1942 I do so not only because I find that period lively and dramatic but because it helps me to express the fullness of what I'm thinking and feeling about the world I live in."[2]

The images Scott evokes and makes use of in telling the epic story of the Raj's decline are drawn from his own emotional involvement in the period.[3] He uses feelings, emotion, and intuition, rather than rely solely on facts, documents, and pure reason. He is, therefore, not presenting an historian's view of the factors that led to the decline and disappearance of the Raj.

Yet, Scott's views on British failure in India can be considered to be an object lesson in historical perspective, because he painstakingly develops conflicting points of view to present the complicated web of cause and effect, to give us a balanced portrait of an incredibly complex picture.

There is Brigadier A. V. Reid with his firm conviction that England was in India for India's well-being, and reciting Kipling's poetry to bolster his morale and that of his battallion. The opposite view, held by District Commissioner Robin White, is that England was in India for what England could get out of it.[4] Reid believed Indians to be inferior and incapable of self-government; White "admired Indians and believed them quite capable of self-government" (*J*, 315). Scott develops both their views with all the subtle nuances within the context of their background and training.

There is Edwina Crane, the English missionary who still hopes that England can recapture her original noble aspirations for India, to recognize her moral responsibility and withdraw from India after the war. To the district superintendent of police, Ronald Merrick, England's morality and responsibility consists in staying in India and getting the job done. To Sarah Layton, Merrick represents the dark, the sad, and the arcane aspects in English life (*S*, 398). To her sister Susan, Merrick is a man to be chosen as a husband.

In Mabel Layton we see an Englishwoman who has lost two husbands in the cause of the Empire; and she seeks refuge behind her rose garden, because the actions of the British Raj have turned into a charade. Her step-daughter-in-law Mildred Layton, on the other hand, tries to cover up her alcoholism and adulterous affairs by sporting a stiff upper lip, and punctiliously playing the role of memsahib to the hilt. To her all is well with the Raj.

There is Teddie Bingham who gives his life to restore the ideal *Man-Bap*, while members of the Pankot English community murmur that it was an act of waste and futility.

There are those, like Sir William Conway, who want to hang on in spite of the death throes of the Raj, and there is Major Clark who cannot wait to get rid of India because it has become a gangrenous leg on England's body, the sooner amputated the better.

There is Daphne, the English girl and Kumar, one of Macaulay's brown Englishmen, wanting to break barriers and come together. But the historic pressures are so strong and divisive that Daphne dies and Kumar is cast adrift as "a permanent loose end."

There is the Congress Party, represented in *The Quartet* by MAK, which has resigned from the various ministries, somewhat impetuously, over the ridiculous point of order raised on the viceroy's declaration of war on Germany. There is Governor Malcolm who believes and supports Indian aspiration for independence, but who is blunt when he tells MAK that the Congress gesture of resigning was a stupid act, which had tacitly given greater reality to the concept of Pakistan and hence moved the country closer to division.

There are over six hundred princes, who had over the years shown their loyalty to the British, now asking Britain to continue her paramountcy and support in a new India about to be born. Lining up against them are the Indian nationalists who consider the princes an artificial creation by the British, their existence unrealistic and anachronistic in the new secular Republic of India.

Adding to the din and confusion are the fanatics from political and religious parties of all shades and opinions, sharpening their knives in pursuit of their narrow parochial goals, not caring if innocent people got slaughtered in the process.

And there are those British individuals, men and women, to whom India had been a home; who had found in India a job, a vocation, a purpose for their lives, now facing an uncertain future as the Raj is about to depart.

These are some of the strands of cause and effect within the tangled web of history that Scott attempts to lay bare for our scrutiny.

History tells no individual tales of ordinary human beings, and Scott has found a remedy for this limitation in his handling of historical facts in *The Quartet*.

There are no charismatic, historical, or political, characters in *The Quartet*. There are references to historical characters but they are distant. They do not come into contact with the fictional characters Scott has created.[5] The characters in *The Quartet*, both British and Indian, are for the most part ordinary middle-class people. They grow and develop within the historical framework and their responses are as individuals.

I *Locale*

If the characters are imaginary, so are the specific locales in *The Quartet*. Except in the concluding volume of *The Quartet* (*A Division*), where the earlier part of the action takes place in Bombay where Guy Perron is stationed, and Sarah is waiting with her father Colonel John Layton to leave for the family reunion in Pankot, and some casual references to Calcutta where Sarah had visited Merrick convalescing in a hospital, all of the action in *The Quartet* takes place in a fictitious world of verisimilitude and dynamic coherence.[6] Mayapore, Pankot, Ranpur, the Bibighar Gardens, Kandipat jail, and the fort at Premnagar, Chillianwallah Bagh, the Sanctuary, Smith's Hotel, and even the princely state of Mirat[7] can only be visited in the pages of *The Quartet*. Yet the structural layout of these places and the intricate hierarchical planning in a princely state are grounded in realistic details.

II *Valuable Source for the Historian*

By drawing upon individual human responses to historic events, *The Quartet* makes the manner in which Britain left India more intelligible than any Indian or British history textbook. In this lies the strength and value of *The Quartet* as history.

In a review of *The Quartet*, British historian Max Beloff considers the novel as a valuable source for the historian, and goes on to say that the historian's techniques, however refined, cannot adequately express "the whole complex of reasoning and feeling that brought about the final debacle of British rule in so incredibly short a space of time."[8]

III *Failure of British Policy*

India was the brightest jewel in the largest empire the world had ever known. For a long time, "since the eighteenth century," Englishmen had said "at home . . . that the day would come when our rule in India will end, not bloodily, but in peace, in a perfect gesture of equality and friendship and love" (*J*, 61). But that was not to be.

After two hundred years, on August 15, 1947, when the British relinquished the jewel and left the subcontinent, they departed with a loss of stature and came to the end of themselves as a people and as a nation. They left after a bitter and tragic confrontation with the people they had governed, leaving behind a divided country as a permanent monument to their policy of divide and rule. This administrative policy, which had been the bedrock of their rule, had turned into their crowning failure.

The subject of *The Quartet* is the failure of British policy in India, the failure of British imperialism.

Scott is concerned with the reasons for this failure. He is concerned with the fallibility of human events that cast their shadow between stated policy and their pursuit and fullfilment; between British aspirations and British betrayals. In order to explore his concerns and map out the area of truth, Scott raised several questions. What were the events and experiences that turned the feeling of love into the violence of a rape? Why, when, and how did the British cease to be *Man-bap* to Indians? Why did the traditionally loyal Indian soldiers begin to question their allegiance? Why did they seek other loyalties so that after taking up arms to fight the king's wars, they turned it against the king to return as prisoners? Why did the noble, cherished ideal of the British to unify India fail? Why could not the British, after decades of rule, prevent the Hindu-Muslim differences from erupting into massive human suffering? Why did their word, recorded in treaties to the Indian princes, become a mere piece of paper with no validity?

IV   *The Historical Framework*

In attempting to answer these questions, Scott was also faced with the basic questions: Where to begin? How much to attempt?

He chose to begin in 1942 for his immediate story, extending it to 1947 when the Raj left. But to account for what took place in 1942, he went back to 1919. This constituted his historical framework.

V   *1919*

In 1919, after World War I, instead of the promised progress toward greater independence and increased participation in the administration of their country, leading toward Dominion status, Indians were subjected to harsher rules governing their lives. The Rowlatt Act and the Defense of India rules provided the government with draconian and dictatorial authority. Suspicion of a possible political act was enough to put an Indian in jail without due process. These regulations were an irreversible setback in the officially stated British policy of gradualism toward India.

Public protests against these measures resulted in greater repression. In the city of Amritsar, in the province of the Punjab, property was destroyed and an English missionary woman named Marcella Sherwood was beaten and wounded by Indians. Brigadier General Dyer of Punjab, a stern official of law and order, deeply imbued with the mystique of the Empire, had a field day with the Marcella Sherwood incident. It was the kind of incident he was looking for, to teach the whole of the province of Punjab, and all of India, a stern and unforgettable lesson. Dyer had his men pick up Indians at random and flog them. On April 13, he arrived in Jallianwallah Bagh where a mass meeting of Indians was in progress, and fired on the trapped crowd. Hundreds were killed and thousands of men, women, and children wounded. For a period of eight weeks following, Indians were made to crawl on all fours where the missionary woman had been beaten. These arbitrary and deliberate actions of vengeance caused grave doubts in the minds of Indians about British promises. Dyer, on April 13, 1919, dealt a death blow to whatever there was of Indo-British harmony, a blow from which it never recovered.

Dyer was mildly chastized for his "injudicious" but overzealous act, and retired on half pay by a parliamentary committee which had enquired into the Jallianwallah Bagh massacre. It was no inquiry, but an exercise in politics. The formalities of British justice had been satisfied, the form kept up.

Scott imaginatively incorporates the Dyer–Jallianwallah Bagh incident into *The Quartet*. Dyer does not make his appearance as a historical character, and the incident on April 13 is not described in any great detail (*J*, 278). But in the character of Brigadier General A. V. Reid, Scott creates an individual with the mind and temperament that Dyer could have had. In Reid's reference to himself as being in a situation similar to the one in which Dyer was, Scott establishes the historical link.

There is also another link established by a reference to Edwina Crane having known Marcella Sherwood. We learn this through Barbie Batchelor. There is no doubt that Marcella Sherwood was on Scott's mind when he created the character of Edwina Crane. Crane is beaten by Indian rioters, but at the same time befriended by an Indian schoolteacher at the cost of his own life. The bitter incident is so traumatic that Crane meets death by fire. By heightening the tragedy of Edwina Crane, modeled on Marcella Sherwood, and shifting Crane's tragedy to 1942, Scott reminds us of the emotional and human impact of the Jallianwallah Bagh massacre.

The significance of the 1919 incident is dramatized even more effectively in Mabel Layton's responses to the Dyer catastrophe. The British in India, in Punjab in particular, raised twenty-six thousand pounds to help Dyer. Mabel Layton refused to be associated with this project. She shocked the other members of

Pankot society with her statement: "Twenty-six thousand? Well, now, how many unarmed Indians died in the Jallianwallah Bagh? Two hundred? Three hundred? There seems to be some uncertainty, but let's say two hundred and sixty. That's one hundred pounds a piece. So we know the current price for a dead brown" (*S*, 61). She sends her check for a hundred pounds through Sir Ahmed Akbar Ali Kasim, father of MAK, to the fund the Indians were raising for the families of the Jallianwallah Bagh victims.

Through Sir A. A. A. Kasim, Scott presents an Indian's view of the Dyer case. Sir Kasim thinks that the Dyer case took place not because of British hypocrisy, but because of British sincerity. He tells his son MAK that the British "have frightened their opponents with their sincerity. I do not mean us. We are not their opponents. Their opponents, the ones who matter but who will matter less and less, are also British. They are men like General Dyer. Why do you call that man a monster? He believed God had charged him with a duty to save the empire. He believed this sincerely that in Amristar there was to be found an invidious threat to the empire" (*S*, 62). He characterizes General Dyer as a frightened person because "frightened persons shriek the loudest and fire at random" *(S*, 62). Then he offers this perceptive comment about the Indians and the British: "Indians are part and parcel of the Englishman's own continual state of social and political evolvement and that to share the fruits we must share the labour and abide by the rules they abide by" (*S*, 63).

Mabel Layton is haunted by the Jallianwallah Bagh tragedy, and during her troubled sleep for the rest of her life, she mumbles and mutters the words "Gillian Waller" which is the twisted and garbled version of the words Jallianwallah Bagh.

The identity of Gillian Waller is a minor mystery to many of her associates, and to Barbie Batchelor in particular. Even after Mabel's death, neither Barbie nor Sarah get a clue to Gillian Waller. It is Scott's oblique and impressively imaginative way of hinting that in this unintelligible Gillian Waller lay the seeds that ultimately grew to uproot the Raj.

VI *1942–1947*

Within the larger framework of 1942–1947 several crucial events took place to accelerate the departure of the British Raj from India. Scott explores, dramatizes, and interrelates these events to show how in their totality they added up to the moral bankruptcy of Britain as a people and a nation, in their handling of their responsibility in India.

VII   *The Quit India Resolution*

British troops were facing reverses in Southeast Asia. Singapore had fallen and the British were retreating from Burma. Japan was making plans to liberate some parts of Eastern India and help set up an independent Indian government. Against these World War II calamities faced by the British, Gandhi addressed the British in his newspaper *Harijan*: "Leave India to God. If that is too much, then leave her to anarchy."

Gandhi's call to leave India to God or anarchy shocked many of his foreign admirers and supporters of India's aspirations for independence. Bertrand Russell was dismayed, and the American press, led by the *New York Times*, expressed concern that Gandhi might "do more harm to his people than Genghis Khan or any other of the long array conquerors."[9] But Gandhi's ultimatum to the British was formalized into a resolution. The All India Congress Committee met in Bombay and on August 8, 1942, passed the Quit India Resolution authorizing Gandhi to take necessary steps to force the British out of India.

In Mayapore, Edwina Crane makes her simple but pointed response. A longtime admirer of Gandhi, she now removes his portrait from the wall. She also stops entertaining Indian ladies to tea.

On August 9, a confrontation between the Indians and the British was unleashed which was to end on August 15, 1947, with the final departure of the Raj.

Using this historic background, Scott incorporates into *The Quartet*, a strong criticism of the repressive measures of the Defense of India rules.

As Robin White angrily remarks, "What in hell was the good of declaring Dominion Status as our aim for India in 1917 and not much more than a year later instituting trial without jury for political crimes and powers of detention at provincial level under the Defense of India rules, ostensibly to deal with the so called anarchists but in practice to make any expression of free opinion technically punishable" (*J*, 322).

It is the rigorous implementation of these rules that becomes the catalytic event for the first volume of *The Quartet* (*The Jewel*). Soon after the All India Congress Committee members passed the Quit India resolution, they were arrested and imprisoned. This action resulted in the violent riots in which Edwina Crane was attacked, and her Indian friend D. R. Chaudhury brutally murdered. The rape of Daphne in the Bibighar Gardens, with Kumar forced to watch the spectacle, was also the direct result of the arrest and imprisonment of Indian nationalists. By dramatizing these two human tragedies Scott heightens the sense of history.

Ronald Merrick arrested and imprisoned Kumar on the charge that he was responsible for the rape of Daphne. When he discovered that Kumar was not *the* rapist, a discovery he would not admit to anyone, possibly not even to himself, Merrick exploited the arbitrary power of the Defense of India rules to imprison and torture Kumar on a trumped-up political charge, namely, that Kumar had had some casual acquaintance with Motilal, a known political activist. Merrick enters Kumar's house, searches his room, and invents false evidence to trap Kumar by planting Daphne's bicycle in a ditch close to Kumar's house. Merrick's actions have the macabre odor of midnight knocks and Kafkaesque incarcerations. Out of such scenarios did the British Raj fashion its justice, to maintain an empire, ostensibly for the well-being of all Indians.

In the deposition of Vidyasagar, a student turned political activist, and in the eyewitness reports of another Indian "Sharma," we are given revealing insights into the inhuman techniques of interrogation and torture used by the Raj to force confessions out of alleged criminals.

In the second volume of *The Quartet* (*The Scorpion*), the arbitrary power of the British is again dramatized in the imprisonment of MAK.

MAK had resigned from the Congress Committee, had not voted for the Quit India resolution, but because he was a member of the Congress, he was also arrested and imprisoned. Governor George Malcolm, meeting MAK just before he is sent to prison, tells him, "There's not a single act committed by you since you resigned office in 1939, not a speech, not a letter, not a pamphlet, not a thing said in public nor overheard in private that warrants your being locked up" (*S*, 17), but because MAK is a member of an outlawed party he is incarcerated.

The Defense of India rules gave the British a legal mask to conceal a dictatorial intention, but in the long run, like the policy of divide and rule, it boomeranged on them, and one result was the birth of the Indian National Army (INA).

VIII   *The Indian National Army*

For generations, Indian soldiers had come down "from their villages in the hills to eat the King-Emperor's salt, to make the regiment their family, the Company, their father and mother and England's enemies their enemies."[10] The British depended upon the unquestioning loyalty of the Indian Army, one of the finest in the world. They had shaped and sustained it over the years into a mammoth unit of defense. The interests of the British from the days of the East India Company had been protected by the Indian Army, and when its men drawn from all over India representing its richness and diversity marched, they took three miles across and eight miles in length.[11] It was their pride and joy, the bedrock on which they had built the Empire.

The rise of the Indian National Army made up of defecting Indian POW's in Asia (Malaya) and Europe (Germany) supported by the Japanese and the Germans was a traumatic event for the British Raj. Phillip Knightley traces the British failure of nerve to this single development.[12] The INA sent tremors of shock throughout the Empire.

The development of the INA and its repurcussions on the Raj's collapse is one of the major themes of *The Quartet*. Scott presents a wealth of carefully researched facts concerning the INA. He is the only British novelist to do so, and his informative background is meticulous. Mohan Singh, one of the founders of the INA, testified to the accuracy of Scott's facts in a letter to the author of this study.[13]

Scott dramatizes and humanizes this development within *The Quartet* in two major cases. One is the case of Sayed Kasim, the son of MAK; the other, the case of Teddie Bingham. Both put their lives on the line for the INA: Sayed, because he sees it as an alternative to the despotic British Raj which has imprisoned his father under the Defense of India rules; Teddie, because he sees in the INA the sinister face of the enemy that is out to destroy the mystique of the empire, *Man-bap*. Teddie gives his life. Sayed is alienated from his father and becomes permanently divided.

In Colonel John Layton, the returning POW from Europe, Scott presents the German wing of the INA. Here too John Layton cannot accept the fact that an Indian soldier can possibly defect to an alien army. In his eyes a national Indian Army is an alien army to an Indian!—so strong is Layton's belief in the British idea of *Man-bap*.

While Teddie Bingham has the courage to go out and meet face to face what the INA has wrought, Merrick reveals the face of a coward. Teddie's actions are what legends are made of, says Merrick. But Merrick himself would seek other cowardly methods to wipe out what the INA has wrought. When an Indian POW in Germany who has defected to the INA is to be interrogated by Colonel Layton, Merrick engineers the suicide of the soldier in question by shaming and insulting him (*D*, 201). Then, to maintain "the human touch" (*D*, 211), Merrick journeys to Pankot with the dead body of the soldier "to tell Colonel Layton to his face" (*D*, 230) that the soldier he wanted to question was dead.

In these encounters and confrontations, Scott again reveals individual responses to historic pressures and makes the complex development of the INA much more intelligible.

IX   *Divide and Rule*

Unity was the often proclaimed aim, but divide and rule was the method used. On the one hand, a physical unity of the land was achieved by the introduction of extensive railroad lines and a telegraph communications system. If these helped the Indians, it helped the British Raj even more in terms of keeping its hand on the pulse of the country, and transporting its troops to troubled spots. Bridges were built, rivers harnessed, and a unified army organized. All this however are merely symbols of "unfinished business" (*S*, 3), because while the Indians learned some skills, they did not share British values or participate as equals in social life. Racial superiority and color prejudice characterized the Raj's policy of divide and rule, an aspect discussed more fully in the next chapter.

"Our only justification for two hundred years of power was unification," says Lady Manners (*J*, 444), and Kumar in one of his letters to Colin Lindsey raises the same issue of India's unification which had been the stated goal of the British: "Isn't two hundred years long enough to unify?" he asks (*J*, 256).

It is true that when the British first came to India in the form of the East India Company, they found a fragmented land. They ruled what was divided and saw in this the opportunity to maintain their power. The gradual encouragement and fostering of these divisions gave them the unique position years later to pose the question: We want to leave. But to whom shall we hand over power? To the Muslims? To the Hindus? To the Princes? To a combination of all three?

By setting up communal electorates, whereby members of religious groups voted for their sects, communalism was legitimized. Instead of the nationalist political organization that Congress intended to be, it became increasingly Hindu dominated, and the Muslim League developed into an organization demanding the division of the country. Communalism had snowballed to such a great extent that division became inevitable. Those who argued against it and wanted to prolong the stay of the Raj at least until this stated purpose of the British, namely, unification of the country, was achieved, were like voices in the wilderness. Those who tried to buck the trend met with death.

The Quartet dramatizes these divisive tendencies and their shattering impact on the lives of people. One such dramatization occurs toward the end in the fourth volume of The Quartet (A Division) and concerns the fate of Ahmed Kasim. Ahmed leaves the safety of his railway compartment to offer himself to the fanatical rioters. "It seems to be me they want" (D, 593) he says, hoping that by his going out, he might avert the larger disaster. He meets his death. We are deeply moved by the death of this one individual as he makes his personal response to enormous historic pressure. Scott uses great restraint in describing this heroic act, thereby adding to the shattering impact. And one can only repeat the rhetorical question of Max Beloff at this point: "What is the sense of studying history if it is not to move one and widen one's moral sensibilities?"

The British support of the Indian princely states was another offshoot of the policy of divide and rule. The six hundred princely states were a varied and odd assortment of principalities. Some were as large as France (Hyderabad), others as small as a handkerchief (Mirat). Some had Muslim rulers with a Hindu majority, others the opposite. Some were ruled through a British resident; others had more direct access to the crown. It was a patchwork of incredible complexity, and the only thing they all had in common was the paramountcy and support guaranteed to all of them by the British.

Scott again dramatizes life in these princely states. He had done it earlier in The Birds of Paradise and in The Alien Sky. In The Quartet he does it within the framework of the State of Mirat with its chief minister, Count Bronowski.

Again the hierarchical levels of protocol, the palace intrigues, the logistics of administering a princely state, are all historically accurate. Scott dramatizes the frustrations experienced by the princely states and the helplessness of the British in keeping their centuries-old pledge to them.

The continued existence of the princely states was an impossibility, geographically and politically, within the framework of the two nations born out of partition. What Scott shows in *The Quartet* is again the tangled web of cause and effect and another instance of British policy failure, of its inability to keep its word to one third of India because its policy of divide and rule had boomeranged and seeped into all levels of the subcontinent.

X   *British Ignorance and Indifference*

The importance of India's natural resources and strategic importance was an acknowledged fact by the British (*J*, 284). England's political and military leaders had declared over the years the importance of India to England's well-being both at home and abroad. Without India there would be no British Empire.[14] India helped create the English middle class, and Colonel John Layton realizing this tells Sarah, "India's always been an opportunity for quite ordinary English people—it's given us the chance to live and work like, well, a ruling class that few of us could really claim to belong to" (*D*, 370). And Guy Perron, looking at English soldiers sleeping in a guard room in Bombay, reflects on India's part in nourishing these men:

> The faces were those of urban Londoners and belonged to streets of terraced houses that ended in one-man shops: newsagent—tobacconist, fish and chip shop, family grocer, and a pub at the corner where the highroad was. What could such a face know of India? And yet India was there, in the skull, and the bones of the body. Its possession had helped nourish the flesh, warm the blood of every man in the room, sleeping and walking. (*D*, 103)

Yet the British, both as a people and in parliament, were indifferent and ignorant about India. When Indian affairs came up for discussion in Parliament, the House of Commons emptied in haste according to Mary Curzon,[15] wife of Lord Curzon, viceroy of India. Lord Linlithgow, viceroy of India, had not even seen an Indian rupee!

In an interview with the author of this study, Scott had expressed several times, feelingly and with some embarrassment, about British indifference to India. "India has always been a crashing bore to the British. I remember Aubrey Menen speaking of a time during the glorious days of the British Raj, when all it needed to get a laugh on the London stage was for a comedian to utter the one word 'India!'"[16]

MAK's father, Sir A. A. A. Kasim, tells his son that the British who really rule them "do not even know where Ranpur is" (S, 63). British soldiers in India are restless and bored when they have to listen to Perron's lecture on Indian history, and Perron realizes how little they cared about a country whose history had been their's for more than three hundred years, and which had contributed more than any other "to our wealth, our well being" (D, 233).

The cartoonist makes fun of British cabinet officials on a fact finding mission in India who cannot make any sense out of a map of India (D, 460). They lack basic knowledge and information about the country they are governing and about whose future they are deciding. This British indifference and ignorance is crystallized in the personality of Aunt Charlotte, Perron's aunt. She is part of the British electorate which had voted for the liquidation of the British Empire. But the vote was cast with neither knowledge nor responsibility, without a thought for the hideous consequences of partition, because "for the majority who voted India does not even begin to exist" (D, 106). Aunt Charlotte, like thousands of other Britishers, feels no responsibility for the massacres that followed, and glibly blames the deaths on "the people who attacked and killed each other" (D, 222). Perron sees in this casual attitude of his aunt "the overwhelming importance of the part that had been played in British-Indian affairs by the indifference and ignorance of the British at home" (D, 222). Such an indifference results in Bunburyism, the phrase coined by Aunt Charlotte for British policy in India, which is no policy at all, or a policy of bungling and muddling through at best.

All previous ideals of unifying the country, imparting values to the Indian instead of only skills, showing moral responsibility and leadership, was abandoned because as Guy Perron notes, getting rid of India would cause no great self-introspection at home because now India had become an economic and administrative burden (D, 222). Thus, withdrawing from India was advanced by a full year, and Lord Wavell, the viceroy who opposed partition, was replaced by Viceroy Lord Mountbatten, who declared in June, 1947, that the Raj would leave ten weeks later, on August 15, 1947.

In this last act of haste, the British gave concrete proof that their interest in India had been purely selfish; that India had served them when they needed her but now keeping India had become a liability. As Major Clark rhetorically asks, "who wants India's starving millions as one of what we call our post-war problems?" (D, 428) the one time jewel in the crown had turned into a curse.

It is in this interpretation of the loss of English ideals in India that Scott expresses his heightened sense of sadness, his strong feeling that in India, the British "wasted a marvellous opportunity" (*J*, 447), and settled for the second rate, "the world's common factor, and any damn fool can teach it, any damn fool people can inherit it" (*J*, 447).

Scott sees in the last days of the British in India a moral bankruptcy, and to him the question of moral responsibility is important. If he narrates the decline within the historical framework, he examines their action "from the moral continuum of human affairs" (*J*, 1).

In mourning the loss of British ideals and the waste of a marvellous opportunity that the British had in India for a positive contribution, Scott can echo the words of Stephen Dedalus, James Joyce's hero in *A Portrait of The Artist as a Young Man:* "I go to encounter for the millionth time the reality of experience and to forge in the smithy of my soul the uncreated conscience of my race."

Herein lies the unique value and significance of *The Quartet* as history.

CHAPTER 8

Race and Class in The Raj Quartet

GUY Perron, a student of Indian history, forever meditating, reflecting, and analyzing British rule in India, acting as Scott's alterego in the concluding volume of *The Quartet* (*A Division of the Spoils*) writes in his journal: "The most insular people in the world managed to establish the largest empire the world has ever seen. No, not paradox, insularity, like empire building, requires superb self confidence, a conviction of one's moral superiority" (*D*, 106).

If insularity and moral superiority helped the British build an Empire, the passionate pursuit of these very same traits resulted in the loss of the Empire as well. Moral superiority manifested itself in racial superiority, and insularity gave birth to Turtonism,[1] to isolation and alienation.

The illusion of racial superiority imprisoned the British in India in their tight little world of narrow perceptions. It inhibited them from reaching out to the larger world of Indian experience and common humanity, and thus wasted the marvellous opportunity they had for becoming a positive force on the subcontinent. Racial prejudice prevented the English from identifying themselves with the Indians, and thus they remained forever aliens under the sky.[2]

To preserve their solidarity,[3] the British drew lines and circles, devised intricate and complex patterns of rigid behavior to conform to the code of the Raj, and erected a network of barriers to keep out the Indian whose land and resources they were enjoying. They expressed their insularity even in their architecture. Walking the streets and avenues of Ranpur, the narrator of *The Quartet* notices that "each road and building has an air of being turned inwards on itself to withstand a seige" (*S*, 13).

Behind the pomp and pageantry of the world's largest Empire, and beneath the rhetoric of Britain's noble aspirations of justice and unity for India, lay England's face of damnation, racial prejudice.

The Indian was an inferior being, and that included all Indians, irrespective of their social or educational background. To use a

Kiplingesque terminology, they were "the lesser breed without the law." It was England's moral duty, "a burden," to civilize the Indian. But in this process of civilizing him, he had to be kept in his place. The best Indian was the Indian servant or the Indian soldier. They knew their place in the system of the Raj, accepted it unquestioningly as an article of faith, and looked up to the Englishman as father and mother—as *Man-bap*. *Man-bap* reaffirmed the superiority of the Englishman, gave him renewed faith in his infallibility. *Man-bap*, with its condescending paternalism, was an important aspect of British racism in India.

The worst Indian was the educated Indian, particularly one who was Anglicized like Kumar. Such an Indian was English in all respects except in the color of his skin. By his very presence, he posed a threat to the Englishman's sense of racial superiority and security. Since color was the one and only certainty the Englishman could hold on to as his badge of superiority, color became the determining factor in the system of the Raj in India.

Racial prejudice is the explosive ingredient behind the tragedy of Daphne and Kumar. In Scott's view, it is also the villain responsible for the Raj's failure, decay, and death in India. Scott dramatizes and lays bare the many facets of race and class prejudice in all their complexity and subtle nuances in *The Quartet*. Sometimes he reveals the nature of this prejudice in a major character such as Ronald Merrick, who aggressively announces his credo when he says that color matters, "It's basic. It matters like hell" (*J*, 391). At other times Scott can reveal it in a simple but telling gesture, as in the meeting between Edwina Crane and the Eurasian teacher Miss William, where the chaplain introduces Miss Crane to Miss William but not Miss William to Miss Crane (*J*, 13); or in the simple attempt by Kumar to purchase a bar of soap in Gulab Singh's pharmacy located in the English section of Mayapore, where English racism is mirrored even in the Indian salesman who subtly snubs Kumar (*J*, 233).

By scrutinizing and coming to grips with Indo-British race relations, "the least attractive feature of the British Raj,"[4] Scott transforms *The Quartet* into a novel of race and class, a penetrating study of colonial racist psychology.

I *"Pre-arranged emotions"*

Imprisoned in the illusion of their racial privileges, the English played out an unnatural and stilted role in India. A self-conscious air of superiority "like a sort of protective purdah" (*J*, 321) became their hallmark. Sarah wants to go back to England before India can corrupt her "utterly with a false sense of duty and a false sense of superiority" (*D*, 354). Every move, every reaction, and every word was expressed with such careful calculation to maintain that aloof image of the Raj that genuine communication with Indians became impossible. In the words of Robin White, "*pre-arranged* emotions and reactions" (*J*, 320) marked the British behavior in India. White blames himself as well for this role playing and admires Mahatma Gandhi who had the courage to think out loudly, "without worrying how many times he seemed to contradict himself, and certainly without thinking of his own reputation, in a genuinely creative attempt to break through the sense of pre-arranged emotions and reactions" (*J*, 320).

Thus the English in India became what Daphne calls "predictable people" with no "originating passion in them" (*J*, 432). "Even when we're alone we're on show aren't we, representing something?" Mabel Layton asks Barbie Batchelor (*T*, 23). When Aunt Fenny tells Sarah, "to establish a relationship with Indians you can only afford to be yourself and let them like it or lump it," Sarah agrees but asks the question, "But out here are we ever really ourselves?" (*S*, 151). This posing that the English feel compelled to do, as though they are on exhibit, takes away their spontaniety. They remain frozen forever in a kind of Edwardian twilight. The English are aware of this stance, for it is a carefully cultivated posture. In Daphne's words, they all work for the white robot which is the British Raj. They will do, say, and believe what it will command, because they have "fed that belief into it" (*J*, 432).

This lack of genuine communication between the Indians and the English, because of role playing dictated by notions of racial superiority, is at the heart of the divisive force in the system of the Raj. It troubles Edwina Crane. She longs to speak freely and openly with Indians because she realizes that "when you chose your words the spontaniety went out of the things you wanted to say" (*J*, 41). To her, genuine, unrehearsed, human communication is the only way by which she could express her sincerity and trust "to people of another race" (*J*, 41).

Thus, when the Indians and the British met, they both acted out their roles, cautiously and guardedly. As Srinivasan says, "behind all that pretence there was a fear and dislike between us that was rooted in the colour of the skin" (*J*, 187).

Because the English played roles, they expected the Indians to play out their roles as well, roles the British assigned them. The stage directions were explicit to the Indians: know your place; know your words; and act accordingly before your masters.

Kumar is one of those who strays from these stage directions and talks back to Merrick, not in the "babu English" which had been the butt of many a Kipling joke, but in perfect English, "better accented than Merrick's" (*J*, 129). Such a deviation makes him the victim of Merrick's racial hostility. Kumar's natural behavior and use of English "like a managing director" (*J*, 237) costs him a job in the British-Indian Electrical Company, but wins for him the insulting epithet, "bolshie black lad" (*J*, 237). Kumar confesses to his friend Colin, "I should start learning how to behave in front of white men" (*J*, 240).

Deviation from his assigned role gets Mabel's old servant Aziz into trouble. When his memsahib Mabel dies, grief-stricken Aziz disappears to mourn her loss in his own private manner. His taking off without explanation, and his reluctance to make his grief public, stirs the wrath of Mildred. She determines to have bloody Aziz booted in the rear when he shows up, and suspects him of stealing silver and even being responsible to some extent for Mabel's death. Mildred is, of course, an expert in playing out the role of a memsahib. It was because her step-mother-in-law Mabel had opted out of the established rules of Raj conduct, that she and Mabel never saw eye to eye. Aziz's behavior is looked upon as an extension of Mabel's attitude when she was alive. But Mildred, true to her role playing, and for the sake of the regiment and the station of Pankot, will not make a crude attack on Mabel, who—when all is said and done—was a memsahib. So Aziz gets the brunt of Mildred's anger both for himself and for Mabel.

Mildred's alcoholism and extramarital affairs; her class snobbery which makes her treat Barbie Batchelor like dirt; and her general contempt for all Indians is concealed beneath her mask of role playing. Putting on her memsahib outfit and accompanied by her secret lover Captain Coley, Mildred goes out on horseback to offer sympathy to the wives of her husband's regiments. She drinks cups of syrupy tea, holds up "squealing black babies" (*T*, 252), and promises hope to the regimental wives of an early return of their husbands from the war in Europe. She returns home in a glow, "but it was external to the affair; a bit too theatrical to the mind where it was needed" (*T*, 252). Sarah sees the real face of her mother behind this facade. "It was an act, but she played the part with a perfect sense of what would be extraneous to it. She did not make the mistake of identifying herself too closely with it. When she came back into the bungalow she shed it, or seemed to shed it and called for gin" (*D*, 345).

Prearranged emotions also resulted in prejudgment of issues, so that the system of the Raj became what Daphne calls "a blundering judicial robot" (*J*, 425). It automatically places Daphne on the side of people who have never told a lie because of the color of her skin. Brigadier A. V. Reid unquestioningly accepts Merrick's version of the Bibighar affair, because Merrick is white and his version is *the* official version. A member of the Raj system can do no wrong. To question Merrick's judgment would be to question English superiority, and go against prearranged emotional responses.

Reid, as a chosen member of the Raj, looks upon his role as one of maintaining the system of the Raj at any cost. Caught up in "the iron system of the Raj," Reid is one of those who would invent a rebellion if the Indians did not start one, "just so that by suppressing it he would feel he'd done his whole duty" (*J*, 315).

Even Merrick, an ardent supporter of the iron system, protected by it and given the freedom to choose victims and twist facts to support his preconceived ideas, allows himself to doubt the fairness of the system. In a rare moment of candor, speaking to Sarah, he uses words to support what Daphne had called the robot like quality of the Raj. "You find yourself automatically implementing a policy you feel passionately is wrong and the only thing you can do short of resigning is detach yourself from the reality of the problem, from the human issues if you like. You become a rubber stamp"; and he continues, revealingly: "I sometimes think that if I'd done something terribly wrong the rubber stamp would have endorsed it. That's it's danger. It's a controlling force without the ability to judge. Once you're part of the rubber stamp process yourself you could almost get away with murder" (*S*, 213).

While there is implicit in Merrick's statement that there might be a possibility of a slipup, there is also the firm conviction that because of that innate racial superiority of the English, no such slipups will occur.

Even at the highest level, genuine communication is hampered by the feelings of racial superiority. MAK finds that he cannot even get the courtesy of a personal reply to his letters from such liberal-minded Englishmen as Governor Sir George Malcolm and Lady Ethel Manners. "He cannot reach them as people: They are protected from him by the collective instinct of their race" (*S*, 39).

II   *The Club*

The most visible barrier erected by the Raj to preserve British solidarity, strengthen the bonds of Turtonism, and keep the Indian out, was the British Club. George Orwell rightly pointed out that the English Club was "the spiritual citadel, the real seat of the British power, the Nirvana,"[5] in any Indian town.

Within the British Club membership was based on the subtle distinctions of the English class system. One club was superior to another, and membership depended upon a variety of factors ranging from attendance at the right public school, to who one married and when.[6] While the club allowed ordinary Englishmen into one club or the other, Indians were barred from not only membership but even as guests of members. When the subject of Indian membership in English clubs came up it "almost split the empire."[7]

In *The Quartet* (*The Day of the Scorpion*), the ruler of Mirat is refused entry to the Gymkhana Club in his own state. He is an invited guest at the wedding of Teddie and Susan, and it is his hospitality which has made it possible for the wedding to take place in Mirat. Yet, because he is an Indian, he is barred from entering the club premises. Even when the awkwardness of the situation is recognized, Mrs. Hobhouse, the colonel's wife, makes certain that no expression of apology be offered and the episode be glossed over as "club or station business" (*S*, 168).

Deputy Commissioner Robin White causes quite a commotion when he takes the minister of education as one of his guests to the Gymkhana Club in Mayapore. The Minister has an impeccable educational background, Balliol and Wellington, shares with the deputy commissioner a love of Shakespeare and Dryden and Henry James (*J*, 179). The members of the club committee promptly take steps to stop White from repeating his social indiscretion" (*J*, 179).

During the war, the club in Mayapore was faced with the ticklish question of granting admission to Indians who were King's commissioned officers in the army.[8] Refusing them "would have been to insult the King's uniform" (*J*, 172). So the English ingeniously devised a system of rules, and a whole set of face saving excuses to permit limited entry to the Indian officers, to the tennis courts outside the club. The bar, the dining room, and the swimming pool became restricted areas. Such an agreement was tacitly agreed to by the Indian officers themselves, who being paid lower than their British counterparts were in no position to keep up their share of the "whack" (*J*, 173).

Even as late as 1964 when the Stranger/Narrator visits Mayapore Club, he is snubbed by the "new race of Sahibs" (*J*, 162), the British expert, because he is in the company of two Indians. The wife of one of the new sahibs, along with her English lady friend, with studied insult snubs Srinivasan by refusing his offer of drinks. In the same breath she asks another Englishman to buy them drinks, "preferring to die rather than have an Indian settle" (*J*, 161).

The Quartet is filled with incidents where racial prejudice within the club takes the form of openly vulgar behavior. British members of the Gymkhana Club empty chamber pots in the swimming pool after it had been used by some Indians and light candles in the pots and set them floating to parody the Hindu religious festival of lights, *Diwali* (*J*, 171). An Englishman excretes into a Gandhi cap and sets it afloat in the pool, and another Englishman, "leader of Mirat's second-fifteen rugger club," breaks wind when the chief minister of Mirat went into the club bar (*D*, 481).

The club was a place for the English to be blanketed "in the colonial warmth of their racial indestructibility" (*J*, 249). It started out as a refuge from their work, but gradually turned into a fortress to be maintained against attack. So as Kumar observes, what started from "the need to protect your sanity," ended up "bolstering your ego and feeding your prejudices" (*J*, 258). To the English the club replaced "the real India" (*J*, 258).

The unreality of club life is emphasized by Daphne when she says, "I felt as if the club were an ocean-going liner, like the *Titanic*, with all the lights blazing and the bands playing, heading into the dark with no one on the bridge" (*J*, 364).

III   *The English Class System*

The class structure is at the very heart of English insularity. According to Scott, *The Quartet* has to be seen as a class novel. "You can't be English and alive without being sensitive to the class problem. . . . I don't think an English writer can write a novel without class being in the background, even if it's not consciously written in; class can't be detached from the English novel."[9] He also believed that the distinctions of the English class system took on an added intensity when they were transferred to India. Thus the "old resentments" (*J*, 131) between the classes in England further complicated the picture of race prejudice in India.

"Money and the lack of it pushed young men towards India"[10] particularly lower-middle-class Englishmen. They made use of the opportunity to become part of the ranking hierarchy and share in the benefits of the Raj's privileged society. To maintain this newfound privilege and retain their status within the charmed circle, they followed and upheld the intricacies and illusions of racial superiority, with all the religious fervor and fanaticism of new converts.

The Quartet is replete with examples of racial insults experienced daily by Indians. Whether visiting a patient in a hospital or boarding a train as Lady Chatterjee does, the ones quick to point out that she be ejected because of the color of her skin, are the English who come from ordinary backgrounds in England. They now have the Indian on whom to vent their hostilities and thereby make up for the subtle insults they had received back home. It is Merrick who cautions Daphne, overprotectively and overzealously, that she watch her step with Kumar, and compliments Sarah mistakenly for keeping the line of segregation with Ahmed, after she returns from horseback riding with him.

Within the enclosed society the English have sought to build for themselves, they play out their own petty dramas of the English class system. Edwina Crane is considered by her employers, the Nesbitt-Smiths, as part of white solidarity and white supremacy, and they "accord her a recognition they would have withheld from the highest-born Indian" but within their "own self-contained society" Crane is relegated to "the lowest rungs of the ladder" (*J*, 6).

Barbie Batchelor, the missionary, faces a similar treatment from her fellow countrymen. Mildred barely tolerates her until the death of Mabel, after which Barbie is thrown out cruelly. Pankot's memsahibs never question her actions, for to do so would be to question themselves, and by implication question the entire system of the Raj.

Both Daphne and Lady Manners, in spite of their upper-middle-class backgrounds, become the untouchables of Raj's English society: Daphne, by bearing Kumar's child, and Lady Manners, by accepting the responsibility to bring up the child.

Memsahibs are the guardians of the English class system in India. *The Quartet* exposes definitively the subtleties of social code and behavior making up the world of the memsahib, and Maisie Trehearne, Nicky Paynton, Isobel Rankin, and a host of others are the arbiters of Pankot's English society. Lucy Smalley, with her ordinary background as a typist and the daughter of a vicar, wants desperately to belong to this inner circle. She eagerly volunteers for

any and all work the various committees have. She even toes the line
in keeping away from Indians of mixed blood, as we will observe
when we discuss *Staying On*,[11] yet the in-society memsahibs do not
quite accept Lucy as their equal.

It is, however, in the characters of Merrick and Rowan that we see
the elaborate drama of the English class system. Merrick comes from
a lower-middle-class background. His parents were poverty stricken
in comparison with the parents of his classmates. As a boy he had
experienced class prejudice. "I doubt there's a more unattractive sight
than that of a school master currying class favor by making fun of the
boy in his form whose background is different from the others" (*T*,
151). Merrick takes to boxing and adds to it his interest in history, to
win for himself a position in the Indian police.

Merrick is aware of his humble beginnings and admires Daphne
for her egalitarian outlook. "Our backgrounds were quite different,"
he tells Sarah, "because mine is very ordinary, but Daphne didn't give
a damn who your parents were or what school you went to" (*S*, 214).

While Daphne is egalitarian, the other English are not so ready to
accept Merrick as their equal. Aunt Fenny, while paying Merrick a
compliment over his fastidious attention to details, calls that 'a sign
of humble origin" (*S*, 141). Sister Ludmila notes the ordinariness of
Merrick's English accent as compared to Kumar's (*J*, 129). When
Merrick wants to marry Susan and thereby gain entry to the charmed
circle, Colonel Layton makes a somewhat apologetic remark about
Merrick not quite belonging to their class. Sarah is much more
vigorous when she says, "He's not quite our class. Class has always
been important to us. Why should it suddenly stop being important?"
(*D*, 365). Sarah also, with the "subtler promptings of the class
instinct" (*S*, 211), recognizes Merrick's lower-class origins in his use
of such phrases as "under the roof" and "not unconscious of the
obligation" (*S*, 210).

Merrick's overzealous championship of the Empire also reveals his
lower-class instincts. Guy Perron, the intellectual who has been to the
right public school, says of Merrick, "Can't the fool see that nobody
of the class he aspires to belong to has ever cared a damn about the
empire and that all the God-the-father-God-the-raj was a lot of
insular middle and lower class shit?" (*D*, 208), and adds that Merrick
suffers from his "middle-class misconception of upper-class *mores*"
(*D*, 209).

Perron, with his "ingrained sense of class security" (*D*, 208), is a
product of Chillingborough and a friend of aristocratic Rowan, but

with the rank of a sergeant he is officially inferior to Merrick. Merrick uses his official position to victimize Perron because of Perron's upper-class background. Merrick takes a sadistic pleasure in arousing Perron's antagonism, because he knows that Perron cannot retaliate. If Perron retaliated, Merrick could punish him with insubordination. He has for Perron "the same tender compassion that is often said to overcome the inveterate slaughterer of game in the split second before he squeezes the trigger" (*D*, 231).

In his treatment of Perron, Merrick gives release to his prejudice against the English class system that had snubbed him as a young man. Yet Merrick, while hating that system, still wants to be a part of it. Since he was not privileged to be born that way, he wants to enter it through the ritual of marriage with Susan.

If Perron's "ingrained sense of class security" offends Merrick and reminds him of his humble beginnings, so does Kumar's Englishness.

In Kumar we see the tragic and ironic results of both the British class and racial prejudice. Kumar is the end product of a declared British policy for India: he is Macaulay's quintessential brown sahib. Observing both his son and Kumar at the dinner table, the Senior Colin Lindsey observes, "But how extraordinary! If you close your eyes and listen, you can't tell the difference. And they seem to talk exactly on the same wave-length, as well" (*J*, 220). Yet in India, because of racial prejudice by men like Merrick and Stubbs, Kumar ends up "a permanent loose end" and becomes invisible to the English.[12]

To Merrick, Kumar is an arrogant westernized Indian who does not know his place. Because Kumar talks back to him, and goes out with an English girl, Merrick chooses Kumar as his victim. More than this, Kumar implicitly reminds Merrick of *his* place. Truth hurts and Merrick reacts aggressively.

Kumar is English by education and cultivation. Perron is English class by birth. Merrick is part of the English Raj officially, "by care and ambition rather than by upbringing" (*J*, 131). This irks him. He is deeply aware that the really classy people, the Laytons, look upon his involvement in the Bibighar affair not as a heroic or patriotic affair, but something to be forgotten. But echoes from that affair—the stone, the chalk signs, parts of a bicycle, the woman in the white saree—keep reverberating to remind Merrick of his involvement. They create scenes, and scenes are definitely anticlass. Thus if Kumar is his victim, Merrick is a victim of colonial ambition.

Black is inferior to Merrick. Black is guilty before the evidence is in. Black and white coming together, for what Daphne calls a deeper communion, is the worst crime there is. Yet the dark holds a fascination for Merrick, casts its spell and makes him long for the satisfaction of his hidden hungers. It is Ludmila who notices the sexual attraction Kumar has for Merrick. Merrick fondles Kumar and gives release to his warped sadistic feelings. Kumar, by his dark handsomeness, "far handsomer than Merrick" (*J*, 129), both attracts and repels Merrick. Merrick wants him, yet does not want him. This ambivalence troubles Merrick's beliefs in his racial superiority and ultimately destroys his illusions.

Even after his marriage to Susan and entry into the higher-class structure the Laytons represent, Merrick's desire for Indian boys continues. He enjoys sex with one of them, Aziz, and luxuriates in a moment of "profound peace" (*D*, 571). But Merrick is disturbed by this feeling of peace, because to admit such peace would be to discard all his firmly held beliefs about racial superiority. So Merrick brutally punishes Aziz, in the hope that Aziz would retaliate, even kill him.

If Merrick reveals the cruder forms of English class distinctions and racial prejudice, Nigel Robert Alexander Rowan, his very name exuding the classy aristocratic and uncommitted aura, reveals the subtler, more refined (and hence more hypocritical?) aspect of English class distinctions and racial prejudice.

Rowan is aware of Merrick's lower-class background. He is so conscious of this distinction that when he finds out that Merrick is about to marry Susan, Rowan abandons his own plan to marry Sarah. The possibility of having Merrick for a brother-in-law, a man who had been associated with the Bibighar affair, is *that* distasteful to him.

Rowan and Perron share a similar upper-class background. Both are public school products. Both share a distaste for Merrick's ostentatious and crude interpretation of racial distinctions. Yet, Perron's egalitarian talk and critical probing of the principles behind the Raj makes Rowan uncomfortable (*D*, 209). So Rowan seeks an ally in Merrick, because Merrick strengthens Rowan's belief in class distinctions.

In his attitude toward Kumar, Rowan again reveals his deep-seated loyalties to his class and race. Kumar's Chillingborough education establishes the school-tie loyalty. Rowan, a man of great sensibilities, realizes that Kumar's version of the Bibighar affair is honest. Rowan is drawn to Kumar. Yet Kumar's accusation of Merrick's sadism revolts Rowan. To accept Kumar's charges, which he knows are true, is to question the justice of the Raj which to Rowan is unthinkable. So Rowan represents what Perron describes as "the comic dilemma of the raj—the dilemma of men who hoped to inspire trust but couldn't even trust themselves" (*D*, 306).

IV *No Place to Meet*

In the British Raj, because of rigidly defined areas for segregated living between the English and the Indians,[13] there were no places where members of both the races could meet and communicate as human beings.

Mayapore had its civil lines for the British and its Chillianwallah Bagh for the Indians. The river separated the two as clearly as possible. Each group kept to their side, meeting either on official business or when the needs of daily commerce brought them into inevitable but minimum contact.

Daphne and Kumar have no place to meet as two human beings to sit and talk. Where to go? she asks, "where people wouldn't have stared and made us self conscious, armed us in preparation to withstand an insult or a vulgar scene" (*J*, 367).

Kumar too agonizes over this problem when he thinks of the possibility of his English friend Colin coming to Mayapore. Where could he have met Colin? The black town is out of bounds to officers, unless they are on official duty. The Gymkhana Club is of course out, for Kumar cannot get past the club gates. At Smith's Hotel there would have been an embarrassing scene because Kumar is an Indian. In the Chinese restaurant no Indian is allowed without the King's commission. The very name, the English Coffee Shop, is to keep Kumar out. They cannot even go to the movies, for Colin would not sit in the seats Kumar is allowed to sit in. "What friendship can survive in circumstances like these?" Kumar asks (*J*, 258).

When Colin does show up, the barriers of race have already come up. Colin does not recognize Kumar, for in India an Indian is invisible to Englishmen.

Race and class, blind allegiance to them, paralyzes British responses in India. Their own self-importance and sense of superiority inhibits and imprisons them. Their rule becomes a charade. Suppressing their humanity, they fail to touch the humanity around them. But if they had forgotten their class consciousness once in a while, and not waved the Indian away as dark, alien, strange, and inferior, the robot Raj would have been given back its humanity.[14]

CHAPTER 9

The Raj Quartet *as Novel*

THE QUARTET is an old fashioned novel in the grand leisurely tradition of nineteenth-century fiction. It is a storytelling novel peopled, with a world of rich and diverse characters, with a beginning, middle, and an end.

To tell a story is, according to Scott, a novelist's key responsibility.[1] At the heart of *The Quartet* is the story of a rape. Why tell this story? There is a story in that answer. There are different versions of the rape and so there are different stories. Each time a character, major or minor, is introduced, there is a story behind that character.

To add to these stories, stemming directly from the central story of the rape, there are several short or side stories. These act as foils to the key stories, to heighten their intensity and set off their brilliance. To mention a few of these: there is the story of the Scottish Nabob MacGregor, the legend behind the gothic MacGregor House in Mayapore, which provides the echoes and ghosts from the past as Daphne crawls to her safety; there is the tragic story of Poppy Browning's daughter who smothered her baby two days after it was born, a dark prophetic undertone to the strange action of Susan who wants to burn her baby in a circle of fire, because the baby "wasn't finished yet" (*T*, 241); there is Count Bronowski's touching tale of "the eighteen-year old English boy who had loved and lost a Spanish girl" (*D*, 147), ambivalent in its subtle meanings but revealing to Rowan, Sarah in love; and there is the sad and anxious story of Lance-Corporal Pinky being victimized by Merrick, one homosexual victimizing another, a profoundly revealing commentary on Merrick's sadomasochism.

With unhurried assurance Scott narrates all these interlocking stories and integrates them into the larger story of *The Quartet*, the decline and departure of the Raj. Therefore, we have stories giving birth to other stories, novels within novels, and "always the promise of a story continuing instead of finishing" (*J*, 450).

The stories emerge because Scott asks questions. The questions, like the stories, are endless. The questions probe and the stories reveal the objective truth that the novelist is seeking—sometimes partially, sometimes totally, but always tantalizingly. He poses the questions and steps aside, letting the characters analyze themselves through word, gestures, and of course through their interpersonal relationships with one another. He never intrudes except to introduce, but he also never abdicates his authority as a novelist to control, organize, and retain the vigor of his conception and the freedom of his objectivity.

I *Narrative Techniques*

Scott uses a variety of narrative techniques to unfold the tapestry of the Raj's death and departure.

In the chapter on *The Raj Quartet as Story*, we have noted the way Scott has made use of letters, excerpts from private journals, court depositions, news items, feature stories, editorials, and even cartoons to give strength and diversity to his narrative.

Scott's characters are passionate, and sometimes, like Barbie Batchelor, compulsive letter writers. Daphne writes to her aunt and Lady Manners writes to Lili Chatterjee; Kumar writes to his friend Colin; MAK writes to the governor and Merrick writes to Sarah, and Sarah writes to Lucy. Scott's use of letters in unfolding the story reminds us of Richardson's *Pamela*.

Scott's characters keep journals. Daphne does it to clarify things for herself. Reid's memoirs and MAK's journals are for posterity. At the end of the day Perron obsessively jots things down, because of his natural inclination as an intellectual with of course the possibility of a scholarly book looming in the future.

Scott is investigating the story of a rape. Like a detective he collects evidence, whether it be a simple entry in a club "members" book or the dusty records of court proceedings. Because he is carrying on investigation against the larger backdrop of historic pressures, news items, editorials, and political cartoons also become part of his technique in the telling of his story.

He is however primarily a novelist, and so reveals the inner emotional turmoil or tranquillity of his characters, through such imaginative devices as dreams and stream-of-consciousness techniques. Barbie's nightmarish dreams of fluttering birds; Mabel's troubled sleep and dark recollections of the Jallianwallah Bagh massacres; Kumar's flights of fancy for the England he loves, as he walks back to his home in Chillianwallah Bagh; and Sarah's stream-of-consciousness monologues, all become part of Scott's narrative techniques.

Then, of course, there is Scott's technique of telling the central story of *The Quartet*, the story of the rape, from several viewpoints. Such multiversions of the same event add fresh insights, give additional information, compensate for the limitations of human perception and communication, and reveal the character of the person giving the version. The different versions challenge our capacity for curiosity and thereby stretch our ability to see more than we originally settled for. It is Scott's technique for getting our total involvement in the story he is telling.

The Quartet is panoramic, with its "slow build up of tension against the background of a war of wildly changing fortunes and then the sudden climax."[2] Its canvas is broad. References to the immensity of distance and vastness of the landscape it attempts to encompass is made in the opening sentence of the first volume of *The Quartet* (*The Jewel*). As *The Quartet* progresses there are constant references and reminders of the Indian landscape which "blankets the mind with an idea of scope so limitless that at times, it is deadening" (*J*, 191). Words prove inadequate to describe such a panorama and "silence is commentary enough" (*J*, 192). To interpret this eloquent silence, Scott resorts to the highly visual technique of the cinema.

It is the shifting wide-angle lens of the cinematographer that Scott uses to give us the sweep and scope of the Indian landscape. It is often the landscape that first looms up before our eyes. Against it, "as if the land were expanding, stretching itself, destroying the illusion that the mind, hand and eye could stake a claim to any part that bore a real relation to the whole" (*S*, 118), we see two specks, blurred images, and gradually the camera focuses, zooms in for close-ups, and as the landscape recedes, Sarah and Ahmed are revealed on horseback. The pattern of the landscape is not visible from ground level, and so we are given aerial views, "God's-Eye views" (*J*, 449) to give us some discernible sense of pattern that has been "hacked into it" (*J*, 449). The wide-angle panoramic camera moves slowly and lingeringly on images—the lush sensual foliage in the Bibighar Gardens; the India of the rains that Daphne loved so much; and stark images of "the panorama of wasteland, scarred by dried-out nullahs" (*D*, 111)—to evoke silently and bring into focus "the strange compelling beauty of India" (*J*, 310).

Thus from the opening frame which projects the key image of *The Quartet*, "of a girl still running in the still deeper shadow cast by the wall of the Bibighar Gardens" (*J*, 1), to the final frame, an aerial view of "dim isolated points of light marking the villages of India that England was leaving behind" (*D*, 598), and the fade out of the plane taking off, with Perron turning off the cameras of his imagination (*D*, 107), Scott consciously uses both the grammar and techniques of the cinema.

The technique of the cinema is also noticeable in the sudden shifting of scenes, and cut backs for contrast, the skillful use of flashbacks, and the freezing of images as tableaux to capture the unique symbols and gestures of characters.

There is Edwina Crane with Chaudhury and the children in her car, singing and driving along the road to Dibrapur. Suddenly the scene shifts and recedes into the background, as the camera closes in on the rioters "spread out across the road" (*J*, 54) waiting to release their violence.

We see Teddie in the Nawab's car going to his wedding reception. We see the stone hurled at the car and catch a glimpse of Teddie's bloodied face and the sense of panic. The scene shifts immediately to the interior of the Nawab's palace where in tranquility the Nawab is "having the frayed end of his coat sleeve trimmed" (*S*, 154).

There is the harrowing scene on the train from Mirat to Ranpur where the camera moves from inside the train to outside it, to show us the faces of people etched in fear within, to the fanatical mob outside consumed by hate and anger. The views shift back and forth with a close up on Ahmed who comes out hoping to pacify, only to be massacred. The impact is devastating.

A mere image often serves, like in the cinema, to make the necessary point, link the stories, bring the past and the present together. Lady Ethel Manners in her black chauffeur driven hearse-like limousine, slowly and silently moving in and out of the streets of Pankot, is an example of this effect.

The freezing of images as tableaux is particularly effective. As he narrates, Scott pauses, often just for a moment, and like the camera can capture that moment to give us a closer look, and imprint on our mind an indelible image. Edwina Crane "sitting in the pouring rain by the roadside holding the hand of the dead Indian" (*J*, 58); Daphne, big and clumsy peering through her thick glasses; Merrick, with his hairy red arms and china-blue eyes smoking his cigarette held between the fingers of his artificial hand; Sarah Layton, standing with folded arms, one hand gripping her elbow; Count Bronowski with his eye patch and limp, with that curious questioning Machiavellian posture; Ahmed, handsome, urbane, but with the clove of garlic; Barbie with her old trunk and no place to go; Mabel with her floppy hat and dirty hands on her knees in the rose garden; all stop and dissolve into the larger scenes.

Scott uses the cinema technique to focus on the microscopic details as well. The camera lets us see the tears in Kumar's eyes as he silently weeps for Daphne; picks out the details of Lady Manners "faded Edwardian elegance" (S, 344); lingers on the Waterman fountain pen of Barbie Batchelor and catches the expression of slight embarrassment on her face from the "faint indelicacy" arising from the insertion and pumping of the pen, to fill it with ink (T, 17); it pauses on Isobel Rankin's index finger as she brings a meeting to order; and effectively makes a statement by a close-up of Colonel Layton's bush shirt hung on the back of a chair, "a mute indication of the grand irrelevance of history to the things that people wanted for themselves" (D, 84).

To the great events of history which form the backdrop of The Quartet, there is a newsreel quality. The images flash: Gandhi being taken to prison; the sounds and sights of a violent war; the brutality of POW camps; Indian soldiers marching side by side with the Japanese; the election of a Labor government in Britain; the mass exodus following the partition of the subcontinent. From these the camera shifts to personal human dramas, as in the case of MAK and his son Sayed. The whole impact of the INA, the divisions within divisions which have become the characteristic features of the Raj, are brought within the confines of a room and made manageable as father and son discuss and debate and reach a point of no reconciliation. The final picture before fade out is on the "muscular geography of Sayed's face" (D, 411).

The technique of looking at a central event from many points of view, reporting it as seen by several different people, reminds us of the cinema technique used so effectively by the Japanese director Akira Kurosawa in Rashomon.[3]

Scott was an ardent student of the theater. He wrote plays for the radio, and nursed a strong ambition to write a play for the legitimate stage. In The Quartet Scott uses several techniques of the stage to strengthen his narrative flow. "Every page should be in a proscenium arch: Well lit, dressed, directed, spoken, filled with action," Scott had said in an interview and had added that in his writings he had sought to "stress the dramatic quality of the novel and the tension at its heart."[4]

We have already noted in chapter 6 the stage-play quality in the episode of Kumar's prison hearing in Kandipat jail. It is a perfect example of what Scott means when he speaks of every page being a proscenium arch.[5]

There are passages in *The Quartet* which read like clear stage settings. Ludmila's descriptions of the confrontation between Merrick and Kumar is such an example. "The Sub-inspector stood . . . his legs apart and hands behind his back. Merrick . . . watching the boy. They formed a triangle, Merrick, Kumar, Rajendra Singh— each equidistant apart" (*J*, 126–27).

When the woman in the white saree, who later turns out to be Kumar's aunt, rushes onto the railway platform in Mirat her actions are described as "an alarming spectacle which, moving as might have been on a stage to an audience already translated to a state of suspended disbelief, could only be a cause of embarrassment on a public platform" (*S*, 20).

When Sarah returns home to Pankot with her father, she sets the stage for her parents to have a reunion and exits. When that "scene was over," Sarah gives herself stage directions: "I can enter now, Sarah told herself" (*D*, 137). When she does enter, physically but not emotionally, she soliloquizes on stage and delivers a monologue.

And Perron in Pankot, at the Layton household, places himself in the position of a spectator, "no more involved than someone in the audience of a theatre." Then he observes, referring to the Layton family, "The play had Chekovian undertones. For all the general air of uneasiness, the uneven cooperative effort to perform, *enfamille*, each member of the cast was enclosed, one felt, by his own private little drama" (*D*, 274).

Even Scott's favorite phrase, "Imagine if you will," with which he prefaces a scene or a character, has a Shakespearean ring to it: words spoken from the prologue in many a Shakespearean play, notably *Henry V*, asking the audience at the Globe to transform the wooden stage to the battlefields of Agincourt.

Like the Greek dramatists, Scott prefers to have his more violent actions off stage. They are reported, and he even uses the memsahibs of Pankot, when they gather to play bridge, to perform the role of a chorus and comment on the action outside, on the news of the war and its impact on Pankot community.

It is in the creative use of the techniques of the cinema and the stage, within the framework of his monumental novel, that Scott makes a significant contribution to the novelist's art.

II *Characters*

An entire book can be devoted to a detailed and fascinating study
of Scott's gallery of characters. Because of the limited scope of this
study, we can only note some of the outstanding features of Scott's
talents for conception and development of character.

We have to search far and wide for a work of fiction in
contemporary literature to match the richness, diversity, and complexity of characters that populate the crowded, but not crammed,
world of *The Quartet.* To find Scott's equal, we have to go back to
Chaucer, who populated his tales with "God's plenty," and to
Shakespeare, who with his sweeping vision from heaven to hell and
hell to heaven filled his world with knaves and kings and all the rest of
humanity in between. Like Shakespeare, Scott too finds in his
characters a mixture of the best and the worst, the ambivalence and
complexity of human nature.

Merrick is a man brutalized by his job. He has a heart of darkness
and, in his tenacity of purpose, reminds us of Conrad's Mr. Kurtz and
Victor Hugo's Inspector Javert. Merrick is a man of rules. Yet
because he is so convinced of the rightness of his cause, he has no
doubts about tampering evidence to fit his cause. Yet Merrick too
retains our sympathy because he is a victim of both colonial ambition
and of the English class system which, by acting as an irritant, makes
him victimize others.

Kumar, a victim of his father's illusions, and who in turn was
victimized by England's false illusions for India, draws our sympathy.
We feel the sharp pain of his exile, are moved by his shuffling gait as
he testifies in the Kandipat jail, and hope that he can someday meet
his daughter Parvathi in the new India and find the peace and
tranquility he had been denied. Yet we become a bit wary of the cloak
of his exile when he begins to luxuriate in that feeling. He begins to
enjoy the role of being an outsider, being trespassed upon, as he
reaches out for a touch of the feel of martyrdom. He enjoys being a
permanent loose end when he describes himself as Philoctetes and
writes his article "Alma-mater." He reveals a note of arrogance when
with English disdain he withholds the gesture of common courtesy to
Lili Chatterjee. He too, therefore, reflects the mixture of the likeable
and the distasteful.

Scott is even more successful in conceptualizing and developing his
woman characters. Edwina Crane, Daphne, Lili Chatterjee, Mabel,
Mildred, Sarah, Susan, Barbie, and all the memsahibs of Mayapore

and Pankot, to mention a few, emerge clearly as a result of Scott's careful study of their personal relationships and private choices. They are examined within the context of time and place in which they exist. Crane's inevitable walk toward her own funeral pyre, *Suttee;* Daphne's genuine desire for deeper communion with an Indian, yet her "curious almost titillating *fear* of his color" (*J*, 372); Lili Chatterjee's own brand of class snobbery as strong as that of the English; Mabel's retreat from the Empire builders of her race, yet her inability to resist the impulse, "to enter the inner sanctuary of the world from which she had cut herself off" (*T*, 193) when she makes one of her rare visits to the Pankot officer's mess; Mildred, deriving her stiff upper lip and her hostilities from Coley and Carew's gin; Sarah, who struggles to identify herself both with her people and Indians, revealing the deep division within her own family and the life of the Raj; Susan's glass-menagerie syndrome and gradual descent into the pits of neurotic melancholy; and Barbie Batchelor, whose brilliant characterization dominates and symbolizes the third volume of *The Quartet* (*The Towers*), a latter day Antigone searching for the proper burial place for her friend Mabel, but ending up with a nervous breakdown, are all individual people, recognizable and identifiable.

Scott's characters continue to retain an element of mystery, the mark of all great literature, long after we have finished reading about them. Kumar and Merrick are two such examples.

Perron did not meet with Kumar, and we continue to speculate about his whereabouts, intrigued about the future of this latter-day Philoctetes.

After nearly two thousand pages, we are still hypnotized, even haunted, by the personality of Merrick. What precisely happened on the night of his murder? Was it the act of one of those programmed within the mystique of a cult with echoes of thuggee rituals? Or did he provoke the boy he had made love to with such brutal sadism that he finally succeeded in making the boy fulfill his death wish? Was there yet another version, even several versions, waiting in the wings to provide further clues, further insights, into the mystery of Merrick, whose life was a dark map of strange obsessions?

Even minor characters receive the same individualized treatment. We remember them whether they be servants like Thomas Aquinas, "who tip-toed everywhere but banged doors so loudly that you jumped out of your skin" (*T*, 9); or Minnie, who rescued young Teddie from the circle of fire to reemerge later on in the pages of

Staying On; or the two tongawallahas, the one with "minute red-veins in the whites of his eyes" (*T*, 246) smelling of garlic, who took Barbie to see Coley; or the other tonga driver who helped her with her trunk from the Rose Cottage, "an enclosed dilapidated man . . . a starved bird with folded wings" (*T*, 367); or Priscilla Begge, cousin of Lady Malcolm, with her look of competence and harassment "with her hockey-player's legs" (*D*, 178).

Scott's characters can be interpreted to symbolize and represent certain imperial or nonimperial archetypes. There are possibilities for a full-length study on such a theme. Primarily, Scott's characters are individuals fighting their private wars and struggling to make their personal decisions based on their individual conscience. While Scott permits his characters to prejudge their fellow characters, he does not exercise that prerogative.

III   *Structure and Rhythm*

"Monumental," "grand," "lavish," "expansive," and "massive" are some of the words that come to our minds as applicable to the structure of *The Quartet*. Although Scott writes about the death and departure of the Raj, there is nothing austere, stark, or hurried about the elaborate epitaph he has engraved. There is, as David Holloway notices, a shambling bulk, hesitancy and repetitions, head-long rushes and *longeurs*[6] built—deliberately—into the framework of *The Quartet* to provide the proper form and structure within which to evoke the ghost of the Raj; to give us the feel of the ponderousness of the Raj as it collapses under its own weight.

Scott had neither charted a blueprint nor sketched a grand design to mount his edifice.[7] Structure and form, like the characters within it, grows, develops, and evolves as the story unfolds. With each volume Scott faced the same problem, "finding a form for what he has to say."[8] "I know where I wanted to go but did not know where to begin."[9]

The four volumes that make up *The Quartet* can be read independently, but to get the total experience and observe the complete intricate structural pattern, the half million word multi-layered tapestry, embellished borders, and all, the four volumes must be read consecutively.

The Quartet is one novel with a four-volume structure. It is one masterpiece—"One huge Veronese scale canvas," as Frank Giles appropriately describes it. On this canvas Scott paints his immense cast of not only his major characters, "but also, like Veronese, household pets and possessions—dogs and horses and rosebushes and a battered trunk and photograph frames and miniature Pathan costume for an European child."[10] And in the character of Perron, Scott paints himself into the picture as well. Only from the proper perspective of distance can we view the entire canvas with all its subtle interplay, color, and light, shadows and spaces, story and symbol.

The Quartet reveals a structure of "architectonic finesse"[11] and the fact that this has been achieved, for the most part unconsciously, is all the more impressive. The four parts of the novel have been so carefully plotted and structured that they interlock with each other with perfect balance and rhythm. It is because of this interlocking quality that characters in *The Quartet* have time and space to grow and develop. It also makes it possible for us to compare the description of a particular scene in one "with the same scene, described by someone else in another and find the result entirely rewarding."[12]

Each of the four volumes that make up *The Quartet* is further subdivided into several parts. Each part, a novella unto itself, has a central image or a character or a group of characters. With subtly orchestrated time shifts, the story unfolds, narrated by a narrator whose identity changes to reflect the events he is talking about. The entire four parts and the parts within these parts are given a unified organic form through certain rhythms.[13]

Repetitions become rhythms in *The Quartet*. Image, character, dramatic event are all skillfully and harmoniously repeated. In the process they take on added meaning, reveal hidden nuances, link the echoes and reverberations of one volume with another.

Scott's stories begin with images. We become familiar with his "Imagine then"; "Picture her then"; "This is the last image then"; and similar invocations to focus our attention on the image. The repetition of his invocations at proper intervals, in itself becomes one of the subtle rhythms in the novel.

There are innumerable images in *The Quartet*, and a detailed analysis of all these images would constitute a study in itself. Within the limited scope of our study we can examine one image, the allegorical picture the jewel in her crown, given to Edwina Crane by Arthur St. John Cleghorn.

The allegorical picture, the jewel in her crown, not only gives the title to the first volume of *The Quartet* (*The Jewel*), but as the novel progresses, its fate reflects the fate of the Raj as well. Edwina Crane packs it away in her chest because it was anachronistic in the India she was witnessing. It belonged to an age when things were "simpler, sort of cut and dried" (*J*, 24). In the second volume (*The Scorpion*), Teddie gallantly and naively attempts to breathe life into the concept of *Man-bap* the picture represented, and in the attempt loses his life. In the third volume (*The Towers*), Barbie resurrects a copy of the picture, but like herself the picture has no place to go. She locks it up in her battered trunk and later gives it to Merrick, who still believed in what the picture represented. In the fourth volume (*Division*), Merrick has given it to his stepson, young Teddie, who tells Perron that everyone in the allegorical picture is dead.

There is an ironic rhythm in the picture ending in the hands of young Teddie. Everybody in the picture is dead. But everyone— including that father he had not seen—who believed *in it* long after that belief was dead, is also dead.

Crane, Teddie, Barbie (return to Crane, because the picture reminds her of Crane), Merrick (return to Crane, because he remembers seeing it with Crane; and return to Teddie, because Merrick was with Teddie when he got killed for what that picture represented), and young Teddie (return all the way to Crane with in between stops), is illustrative of how Scott has created these rhythms and skillfully linked one volume to another. A similar approach can be applied to other images as well to discover the manifold rhythms in *The Quartet*.

The Quartet is a complex and sustained work of the imagination on the universally important theme of the personal relationships between people of different cultures and races, against the background of historic pressures. It is the consummate work of a superb novelist who brings to his work a wide range of talents: the innovative use of a variety of narrative techniques; a firm grasp of the various strands in the dense jungle of Indo-British history; an awesome emotional range for characterization; a vivid imagination for integrating image and story and a facility of prose style that can be precise and direct or lavish and elaborate like a rare piece of Indian sculpture. It is, however, Scott's moral intensity, his telling of the epic story of *The Quartet* "within the moral continuum of time," that lifts the novel from a major work to a masterpiece.

The Quartet is one of those rare works that yields fresh new insights and new textures of meaning each time it is read, and continues to maintain the aura of mystery and ambiguity, the hallmarks of great fiction. It is a work of lasting greatness, and the fact that Scott "was able to bring it out within less than ten years ranks as very nearly a literary miracle."[14]

CHAPTER 10

Staying On: *A Postscript to* The Raj Quartet

THE successful completion of *The Quartet* brought personal satis-faction to Paul Scott. But with it also came a feeling of anti-climax, a letdown felt by most writers when a major work is completed. Scott thought he had written all he possibly could about the British Raj, which had become his "home" for these ten years and more. Like one of his own Anglo-Indians, he was now confronted with the question of where to go as a writer: To England? Or stay on in India? He wanted to leave India behind, but that was easier resolved than executed. As John Willey, Scott's New York editor pointed out, Scott had been so completely at home in India, emotionally and psychologically, that the change was not going to be easy.[1]

Scott therefore opted to stay on, a bit longer anyway, before finding another "home." *Staying On*, which is written in a terminal tone, is his touching and reluctant farewell to India, a most appropriate postscript to *The Quartet*.

After completing *Staying On*, he had remarked that he had said all he had wanted to say about India and would not write anything more about her. The anxiety caused by this statement among his readers was best expressed by Frank Giles when he wrote, "Paul Scott now intends to give up writing about India. This is like hearing that Sir George Solti will never again conduct Strauss, or that the Rothschild family will no more make vintage wines from their Lafite vineyard. For the sake of your admiring, and now surely increasing, public, think again, Mr. Scott, think again."[2]

Had Scott begun to think again? Had India released yet another story-behind-a-story which he was eager to tell? Was he anguishing somewhat like his fictional creations, for example, like the novelist Edward Thornhill in *The Corrida at San Feliu*, restlessly taking his characters with him wherever he went, to find them a locale? Was there in Scott at this point a compelling desire to demonstrate that he could write about other places and other people? Was Scott feeling somewhat like a typecast actor wanting to break out, to stretch himself with other roles, other psyches? We can only echo Scott's own ideal novelist and ask questions, "questions unsusceptible even of formulation."

Scott had, however, begun another novel, "just a few pages. One cannot watch television all the time while lying in the hospital bed,"[3] he had said to the author of this study. Because Scott was one of those few novelists who talked about their work only after it had been completed, the author of this study restrained his curiosity from finding out what these "few pages" were about. Later inquiries only revealed that Scott had had two possible titles in mind for this new novel. *Mango Rain* was one, a very Indian sounding title. *A Man and his Two Daughters* was the other, which could be Indian, English, or any other. It is our irreparable loss that he did not remain to complete it.

Are you staying on? Or going home? These were among the frequent questions asked by Englishmen of each other during the days of the British Raj; and these questions assumed a sense of urgency when the departure of the Raj became inevitable.

Many Englishmen had to make a decision about where "home" was. Was it England's lush-green pastures and quiet Tudor homes in tranquil Surrey or Sussex? Or was it in India, where they had stayed and worked at a job that had given meaning to their life sometimes for several generations?

Some English families made a trip home before deciding on "home." Others relied on letters and firsthand reports. There were not only questions of readjusting to England's cold climate but of finding new roots, for the England they had left was not the England they were returning to. There was of course the more practical question of how far one's India pension could be stretched in England. Considering all these questions where would one stay if one did? India? Pakistan? Where would one's loyalties be? One's sympathies? One's roots? India or England? India or Pakistan? For many English families it was a hard and emotional decision to make.

Some went home to England only to be disillusioned, to return and stay in India like the Anglo-Indian colonel in Rupert-Croft-Cooke's novel *Another Sun, Another Home*. Others, like the Blackshaws in *Staying On*, had tried to remain by planting tea, but had given up and gone home. Then there are the Peabodys in the fourth volume of *The*

Quartet, A Division (*D,* 573), who opt to stay in Rawalpindi, Pakistan.

In the first volume of *The Quartet, The Jewel,* we come across the phrase "staying on." Edwina Crane, when faced with the question after her initial three-year stay, decides to stay on (*J,* 11), and she does so for the next thirty-two years until her tragic death.

Some Englishmen and women chose to move to other British colonies, in search of the colonial life they had grown accustomed to in India.

In *The Alien Sky* Cynthia Mapleton decides to go to Kenya and admits uninhibitedly, "I have a taste for being waited on by coloured servants" (100). But to Tom Gower, the idealistic Englishman, leaving India would be like committing suicide, for he has found in India a job that has given his life meaning and purpose. Sir Robert Conway, in *The Birds of Paradise,* makes a last ditch effort to back up a stand for independence by the Maharajah of Gopalakhand, so that he can stay on and continue his job as adviser to the Maharajah, for the Conways were bone of India's bone. When this fails, he stays on anyway, hoping to write his memoirs. Ronald Merrick of *The Quartet* had planned to stay on, if not in India at least in Pakistan. Nigel Rowan is another Englishman from *The Quartet* who wanted to stay on by working out a private contract of service with Bronowski and the Nawab of Mirat after the Raj had left. The Raj's departure not only uprooted many Indian lives in the mass migration, it uprooted many English lives too, making them immigrants in a land they had taken for granted.

These people who stay on, these permanent exiles, form a subculture of their own all over the world. Malcolm Muggeridge perceptively comments on this group. "They are survivors, of whom in changing times like ours there are so many and so varied, to be found all over the place—strange wizened mandarins staring in front of them in Peking, aged English governesses eking out some kind of existence in Rumania or Hungary, irritable Brigadiers with red faces mowing their lawns in the home counties of Southern England, penurious aristocrats haunting draughty ancestral residences."[4]

I *Lucy and Tusker*

To this group of permanent exiles belong the Smalleys, Colonel "Tusker"[5] Smalley (Indian Army, retired) and his wife Lucy (Little me) walk-on characters in the crowd scenes of *The Quartet.*

We are briefly introduced to Lucy Smalley in the second volume of

The Quartet (The Scorpion). She is at a bridge and tea and plenty-of-gossip party attended by the Pankot memsahibs. It is such a brief appearance by Lucy that if we "blinked" we would have missed her.

Our next encounter with the Smalleys is in the third volume of *The Quartet (The Towers).* Lucy, with her shorthand skills, is asked to be secretary of an emergency committee. She readily accepts even though she is secretary to three permanent committees, because she is "a glutton for work" (*T*, 48). Both the Smalleys are then introduced:

Most stations had their Smalleys. . . . Because they looked nondescript and unambitious they provoked no envy and hardly any suspicion. In Pankot, where they had been since the end of 1941, they arrived at parties harmoniously together and then put distance between them as if to distribute their humdrum selves in as many parts of the room as possible. Leaving, they did so arm-in-arm, giving an impression that by playing their separate parts in a communal endeavour something integral to their private lives and mutual affection had been maintained. (*T*, 48)

They are "slight bores but very useful people" (*T*, 48), and they lived in Smith's Hotel where they went well "with the napery and the potted palms" (*T*, 49); and while their personal arrangements were always breaking down as not having a lift home after a party, "they always managed to get one" (*T*, 48).

In the fourth volume of *The Quartet (A Division),* we learn that the Smalleys have rented Rose Cottage from the Laytons, and that because Tusker is too young to retire and "a bit too old to fancy his chances at home" (*D*, 492), he has agreed to stay on for a year or two at least.

Tusker and Lucy are center stage in *Staying On,* just as Lucy had always wanted.

Tusker and Lucy are the last of the withered "survivors of Pankot's permanent retired British residents" (15) and have risen to the stature of a tourist attraction for American tourists who wanted to see "old style British" (73) still around.

The time is April, 1972, twenty-five years, a quarter of a century since the British have left the subcontinent. They had carved two nations out of one. Now there is a third one, Bangladesh. Colonel "Tusker" Smalley is now seventy. For a couple of years, soon after independence, Tusker served as an adviser to India's new army from which he retired. Then, for about a dozen years, he had a commercial job with a firm in Bombay which had sent him to London on a short business trip in 1950. Lucy had gone with him, her first home visit in over forty years. Tusker retired when he was sixty, and he and Lucy have been back at the small hill station of Pankot, where they had lived during the heyday of the British Raj.

II *"Hanging on"*

Lucy and Tusker are staying on, or "hanging on" as Tusker admits in one of his many moments of truth, at the Smith Hotel or rather in its annex, the Lodge. They have one servant, Ibrahim, because that is all they can afford. Ibrahim, who comes from a family that had served British Sahibs, is himself "England returned." Also part of the Smalley's household is "Bloxshaw," the dog left behind by the Blackshaws.

Smith Hotel is owned by Mrs. Leela Bhoolabhoy, a Punjabi woman of mountainous flesh who is married to her third and youngest husband who was "constructed on more meagre lines" (2). Francis Bhoolabhoy, "a cradle Christian" or Billy-Boy, as Tusker calls him, is "management," while Mrs. Bhoolabhoy is "ownership," terms by which they address each other when Mrs. Bhoolabhoy is in an irritable mood, which is most of the time. Their marital mishaps and occasional "combined and gigantic climaxes" constitutes the subplot of *Staying On*, a perfect counterpoint to the equally humorous and sad happenings between Tusker and Lucy.

In postindependent India while Tusker Sahib and Lucy "mem" are still Colonel Sahib and Memsahib to their longtime Indian servant Ibrahim, they are no longer in command. 12 Upper Club Road (the former Rose Cottage) is presided over by Colonel and Mrs. Menektara, and Tusker's savings cannot be stretched too much longer. His past Raj connections and white skin are no longer the valid passport to the world of privilege.

In fact, the Smalleys are about to be dislodged by Mrs. Bhoolabhoy who has been cooking up her private plans to develop Smith's Hotel. She has decided to sell out to the Punjabi Syndicate that owns Pankot's new five story and concrete hotel, Shiraz. The moment that deal is consummated, Smith's will be torn down, a secret she has kept even from her husband, Francis Bhoolabhoy.

She orders her husband to write a strict letter to Colonel Smalley, telling him to look for another place. Francis Bhoolabhoy is reluctant to write such a letter because he is fond of Smith's and fond of Smalley. But his wife's threats and anger prevail and Bhoolabhoy complies. The crude letter giving the dreaded news is tantamount to deportation, which in a symbolic sense it is, proves fatal to Tusker who has just been on the mend after an illness. Clutching the letter, Tusker collapses among the bed of canna lilies, his favorite flower, and dies of a massive coronary.

The novel begins and ends with Tusker's death. Through a series of flashbacks and a mastery of the antichronological time sequence for which Paul Scott is famous, we get the sad, ironic, and always hilarious portrait of the Tuskers and a host of other characters with whom they come into contact. Once again, Scott uses letters, reminiscences, and a variety of other people's viewpoints to reveal their dim, disappointed lives.

Tusker, like a true Englishman, has begun falling physically apart with all the customary attention to detail, as if fitting himself in advance for his own corpse to make sure he was going to be comfortable in it (21). Lucy realizes this and is frightened at the prospect of becoming a widow, alone in a foreign land.

Tusker needs an "irritant" to keep him alive and kicking. He uninhibitedly uses Ibrahim to blow off steam, keeps giving him the "push" at the slightest lapse of duty and "reinstates" him equally fast. Then, of course, there is the privately printed *A Short History of Pankot* by Edgar Maybrick (Barbie's friend from *The Towers*) which Tusker rips apart by spotting what he thinks are mistakes. But Tusker's single biggest irritant is Mrs. Bhoolabhoy who, when Tusker was ill and flat on his back, had fired the Mali. With the Mali gone the grass has grown thick and "jungly" in front of the Lodge. Tusker flies off into a rage and Lucy uses all her skill to calm Tusker. She and Ibrahim mount "Operation Mali" to pacify Tusker.

Then there is Lucy herself, an English clergyman's daughter (mother, Emily Large; father, Matthew Mark Little), a former typist who, with her ridiculous habit of adding "Little Me" whenever she referred to herself, has had a sad life.

"From the beginning I had a sad life," she says: "A life like a flower that has never really bloomed" (67). She daydreams. In her moments of deepest solitude and despair and on days when it has been impossible to live with Tusker, she summons up her secret lover from the depths of her past. He is Toole, "a local man, the son of a ploughman on one of uncle Percy's farms" (168). Over the years he has always been with her on the periphery of her fantasies but as she has grown old and weak, he has become younger and stronger and visits her more often. She makes him up with her identikit, giving him the eyes of a Paul Newman or a Steve McQueen, depending on the movie she has seen. Then she plays for herself her favorite record, Dinah Shore singing "Chloe."

It is not the past that worries Lucy or about which she complains. She is frightened about the future. In a moment of uncontrollable fear and rage she asks Tusker to tell her what her financial position would be if he should die before her and leave her alone. She stuns Tusker into silence.

In reply Tusker writes her a letter clearly outlining his financial position. It is his last will and testament and the detailed accounting he presents reflects, as it did in *The Bender*, Scott's intimate knowledge of accounting from his days as an accountant. But it is in this letter that we get the real reason for Tusker staying on.

Tusker cannot think of India as a place where he merely drew his pay for the first twenty-five years of his life. It is a place where he had invested *himself*, where he had been happy doing his job (195–96). Or as Lucy puts it, "Tusker liked working with Indians. And because he was happy he was good to me" (141).

In these words of Tusker and Lucy, Scott again restates his important theme of men and their relationship to their jobs.

III *Ibrahim*

Tusker needs his irritants. Lucy needs her Mr. Toole. Lucy and Tusker both need Ibrahim. In a rare moment of honest confession, Lucy takes Ibrahim's arm and says "dear Ibrahim, what should I do without you? What would either of us do?" (39).

Ibrahim is a marvellous creation. Scott shows remarkable understanding of the Indian world of servants in his delineation of Ibrahim. Like old Joseph, the servant of Edwina Crane in *The Quartet* (*The Jewel*) who is proud that his mistress is a memsahib, Ibrahim for all his fights with Tusker still looks upon his position with the Tusker family as a status symbol. There are times when Tusker is not talking to him; times when Lucy is not talking to him; times when both are not talking to each other but *only* through Ibrahim.

Ibrahim is constantly amazed at the flexibility of the English language he hears around him in the Tusker household. In Ibrahim's use of English, Scott has captured the idiom, the richness, resonance, and comedy of the English dialogue as spoken by Indian servants "tutored" by Sahibs of Raj times. "What is Sahib taking me for?" demands Ibrahim. "Day tripping bugger fellow?" (28). "Bugger" is a favorite word of Tusker, and his constant usage makes it a permanent part of Ibrahim's lexicon. He has a high opinion of his own English as he corrects the Mali, "If you hope to go foreign you must learn pukka English" (13).

It is also Ibrahim who maintains complete impartiality, as far as the motley human parade is concerned. To him, Sahibs, Muslims, Brahmins, Western-Punjabis, Banyas, Bengalis, and Rajput princes are all, "bugger fellows" (203).

On the sly, Ibrahim carries on with Minnie, whom we remember from the second volume of *The Quartet* (*The Scorpion*) who has now grown plump and grumpy. It was Minnie who had rushed to rescue young Teddie from the circle of fire lighted by his mother Susan. Minnie is now Mrs. Bhoolabhoy's personal maid.

IV   *Minor Characters*

Other minor characters in the novel are sharply etched and add to the comedy and sadness of the total picture. There is Reverend Stephen Ambedkar ministering to the "spiritual needs of Pankot's Christian community" (101), who took a generous swig of wine "left at the bottom of the chalice" (101) when he administered but a drop to those who came to church; and his assistant Father Sebastian, of "such dense blackness of skin it showed purple" (104), an Anglo-Catholic who irritates Susy—who would much rather be damned than play piano "for a minister who wants to be called Father and is as black as two hats, especially in a church he wouldn't bring me to" (105).

Susy Williams is a Eurasian, "born chapel," mother Indian but father English. She is the oldest acquaintance of the Smalleys in Pankot, and does Lucy's hair by visiting the Lodge once a month. Now she is working in the Seraglio room of the Shiraz under the direction of Sashi, "trained in Mayfair, London wearing his wet-look black trousers" (176). Although Lucy likes Susy, she is still troubled by Susy's color because Lucy finds it difficult to forget the early lesson memsahibs were taught by other memsahibs, "to steer clear, socially, of people of mixed blood" (172).

V   *Links to* The Quartet

The earlier and larger world of *The Quartet* impinges on the smaller world of the Smalleys in *Staying On*. Echoes from the past keep coming into Pankot. A letter from Sarah Layton to Lucy commenting on the death of her father James Layton, her marriage to Guy Perron, now a professor of history, and the introduction of a young Englishman David Turner, links the two worlds.

Turner's visit to meet "English people who stayed on" (77) and to look over "old British gravestones" (77) provides an opportunity for Lucy to indulge in one of her imaginary conversations, her soliloquies.

In the hands of a lesser writer these soliloquies, by both Lucy and Tusker, would have sounded very contrived. Scott handles them convincingly and naturally. Lucy and Tusker are old, on the edge of senility, and talking to themselves or to imaginary people and wandering between the corridors of fact and fantasy is as natural to them as the aches and pains of their creaky old bones.

VI   *A Sad Comedy*

The conclusion of *Staying On* intensifies the sadness of Lucy and Tusker's life and reaches a poignancy when Lucy cries out, "Tusker, I hold out my hand and beg you, Tusker, beg you to take it and take me with you. How can you not, Tusker? . . . How can you make me stay here by myself while you yourself go home?" (216).

Staying On is a superb novel by a writer who was at the height of his powers. It reveals Scott's compassion and dry humor; a sureness of place and people; of dialogue and drama, as Lucy and Tusker emerge as two very identifiable people.

To those who have read *The Quartet*, *Staying On* will have added significance. To those who have not, it will whet their appetite to read *The Quartet*.

Staying On won England's most prestigious award, the Booker Prize for fiction for 1977. Allan Furst writing in the January, 1978, issue of *Books and Bookmen* stated, "for the first time I have no quarrel with the judges." Frank Giles complimented the Booker jury on their taste and wisdom.[6] Scott was unable to attend the dinner at Claridge's to accept the prize in person, for he was recovering from an operation in Tulsa, Oklahoma.

About a year earlier, in reviewing a book by another Booker Award winner, Scott had commented on the Booker Prize: "It is an author who gets the prize, not a book, and in choosing an author a very complicated range of sensibilities and attitudes is obviously brought to bear," he wrote, and added, that even in selecting a book, the judges take into consideration the whole body of an author's work. "I do not quarrel with that, I am all for it. But let them say so. And when it comes to choosing a first novel (I think it has happened only once) let them make it clear that it is not at all a question of "best" but of excitement over the sound of a new voice (a rare phenomenon)."[7]

When *Staying On* won the award there was a general feeling that the award was a belated acknowledgment of Scott's sustained literary accomplishment culminating in *The Quartet*.

CHAPTER 11

Paul Scott: Summing-up

T HE British in India is Scott's territory. From his first novel *Johnnie Sahib*, where young, brash Johnnie Brown wears the mantle of *Man-bap* as securely as the color of his skin, to his terminal novel *Staying On*, where Lucy and Tusker, survivors of the Raj, hang on for dear life, Scott exhaustively mined this vast territory and distilled its nearly two hundred years of experience. In between his first and last novel, Scott made three attempts to get away from India, but, to use one of his own favorite phrases, India was always at his elbows like an invisible presence. Even in the non-Indian novels, the echoes and memories of India kept intruding.

In selecting the British experience in India as his major theme, with many variations, Scott took on the biggest theme open to British writers. In the opinion of Anthony Burgess, "since the Victorian giants—who were all Fieldingesque picaros anyway—we've only had one block busting theme, and that was the rise of the British empire. It's a theme that's been merely nibbled at, Kipling—who could have written an Anglo-Indian *War and Peace*—being the most shameful nibbler of them all. We're stuck with our muffled curses at the welfare state and our exhausted records of adultery in Hampstead."[1]

"In heroic contrast to the rigamaroles of modern fiction,"[2] Scott's *The Quartet* is an Anglo-Indian *War and Peace*. His picture of the Raj is so total and complete that Webster Schott, writing in the *New York Times*, said, "I cannot think of anything worth knowing about the Raj that Scott hasn't told me."[3]

I *Place*

It is difficult to place Scott in the context of any literary tradition with reference to his non-*Quartet* novels. They have two things in common. First, all of them express Scott's metaphor for revealing his personal view of life, namely, men in relation to their work. Second, in all these novels Scott was either consciously or unconsciously warming up to the major work of his writing career, *The Quartet*.

The Corrida at San Feliu; *A Male Child*; *The Mark of the Warrior*, and *The Birds of Paradise* are superb novels both in crafstmanship and characterization. *Johnnie Sahib* and *The Alien Sky* are at the opposite end of the spectrum and mark the two weak spots in Scott's writing career. *The Love Pavilion* stands between these two groups. If Scott had not lost control of his story about Saxby and Tom Brent and avoided the heavy-handed symbolism, *The Love Pavilion* could have joined the first group of superb novels. *The Bender* stands by itself as an enjoyable novel, revealing Scott's talent for the light and humorous touch.

We have no difficulty in placing *The Quartet*. It is written in the grand tradition of nineteenth-century fiction. With his keen sense of history, broad panoramic canvas, a crowded world of rich and diverse characters, and a heightened sense of moral intensity, Scott is in the mainstream of Tolstoyan tradition. *The Quartet* is the Anglo-Indian *War and Peace*.

While in the Tolstoyan tradition, Scott is also close to and concerned with what Peter Green calls "the Jamesian obsession with the minutiae of emotional betrayal." The dying British Raj was appropriate for such Jamesian introspection. The Raj had "a subtly corrupted ruling class with enough leisure. . . . Yet enough blind self-assurance to hold firm, set over an ancient sophisticated society torn between religious primitivism and radical politics."[4] And Scott, like James, took his writing seriously and was immersed as "Henry James in the study of his chosen world,"[5] rigorously keeping his pictures within the limits of a frame, choosing his "center of composition," handling his "perspective," and turning on the "lights to reveal those fine perceptions"[6] of thought and character.

Scott also has kinship with Conrad, whose writings he greatly admired. We see in *The Quartet* something of the panorama of the large canvas of *Nostromo*, "the whole of a vast, imagined republic, where all humanity's passions, meannesses and failures from ideals may run riot." Writing to H. G. Wells, Conrad wrote, "I am but a novelist. I must speak in images."[7] Conrad "frequently used what may be called a 'controlling' image, that is, an image which both controls the plot and theme and reveals psychological aspects of character."[8] We have noted how Scott begins with an image, repeats it, and achieves both narrative impact and revelation of character. Like Conrad, Scott believes in a good story as the heart of a novel, that a story should be accounted for, and uses, like Conrad in *Lord Jim*, three or four storytellers in a single novel.

The Quartet also brings to mind Ford Madox Ford's Christopher Tietjens tetralogy, *Parade's End*. Built on an immense scale, Ford wanted "the novelist to appear in his really proud position as historian of his own time,"⁹ in this tetralogy. This "four volume meditation over the coming apart of the British Empire"¹⁰ bears favorable comparison with Scott's work. Ford writes about a crumbling world and deals with "shifts in both space and time and with a theme that could be handled adequately only by a sequence novel of a length commensurate with the changes it represents."¹¹ In the use of techniques, in the portrayal of desperate human situations against a background of social, moral, and political upheaval, there is much in common between *The Quartet* and *Parade's End*. An independent comparative study of the two tetralogies would be rewarding.

Among contemporary writers, Scott admired Graham Greene, and in a letter to the author of this study had expressed his feeling that if any British writer deserved the Nobel Prize, Greene did.¹² We notice in Scott's writings some stylistic similarities with Greene.¹³

It is inevitable, almost axiomatic, that any British writer who writes about India be compared with Kipling and E. M. Forster.

In spite of Anthony Burgess's hope, Kipling could never have written the Anglo-Indian *War and Peace*. Kipling was a miniaturist and lacked the sustained open vision and psychological introspection for taking on such a theme. His attempts at novel writing were not very successful. *Naulakha*, a novel set in a princely state, is sophomoric when compared with Scott's brilliant *The Birds of Paradise*, which has a similar background. Kipling's *Kim*, at the time it was written, was a good novel, but it is essentially a boy's adventure tale. Kipling celebrated the glory of the Raj, Scott mourns the loss of British ideals. Kipling accepted the Raj, warts and all. Scott probes, questions, and analyzes the Raj. Kipling's India writings are mere footnotes in relation to Scott's India novels.

Scott had to write for too long a time in the shadow of E. M. Forster. Forster's one Edwardian novel, *A Passage to India*, attracted a large following. It is a good novel and, within the framework of Indo-British relations, explores the larger world of personal human relationships. Peter Green appropriately sums up the relationship between Forster's *Passage* and Scott's *The Quartet*: "By his choice of central motif Scott, deliberately it would seem,

challenges comparison with *A Passage to India*. He can well afford to
do so since Forster's work looks parochial, if not superficial, by
comparison."[14]

II *Rank*

It is as a novelist that we have to evaluate Scott. His attempts at
poetry and plays were peripheral. As a novelist it is *The Quartet* and
its postscript *Staying On* that becomes the deciding factor. It is so
enormous that it overshadows the rest of his writings.

When Webster Schott sums up Scott's contribution to literature as
permanent, and Phillip Knightley calls Scott's work "a literary
triumph of the highest order,"[15] and Max Beloff calls Scott's
achievements "a major one,"[16] and H. R. F. Keating declares that
the Titanic struggle on the subcontinent found a superb chronicler in
Scott,[17] they are all invariably referring to *The Quartet*.

There has been a unanimity of critical praise for Scott's major
work. Criticism has mainly focused on the length of the work, the
elaborate details, the embellishment within the embellishment. What
Scott has done is to give the actual feel of people and events in India.
Length is part of the epic story necessary to unravel thread by thread
the tangled web in which the Raj found itself. He seems to be writing
not just for our times but for posterity, like some of the nineteenth-
century novelists whose tradition he continues.

Far superior to Kipling and Forster, Scott is close to Tolstoy and
Henry James, to Conrad and Ford Madox Ford. Scott has now set
standards against which all writers of the British experience in India
will have to be evaluated. He has successfully incorporated into
English literature the Indian experience. In the words of Benny
Green, "The melodrama which opened *The Moonstone*, with the
British first becoming aware of the jewel in the crown, now ends with
The Raj Quartet, as they mourn its irrecoverable loss."[18]

The diversity of *The Quartet* is its strength. To the student of the
novel, it is rich with the technique and craft of the novel. To the
historian it is a valuable source, and for the humanist it is a highly
perceptive commentary on interracial, intercultural relations. To the
student of the performing arts there is a gallery of characters to bring
to life, and to the general reader it is a series of novels within novels to
read and enjoy. Its stature as a major work of fiction will grow and
endure in the years to come, and so will the reputation of its author,
Paul Mark Scott.

Notes and References

Chapter One

1. John Leonard, "Private Lives," *New York Times*, March 8, 1978.
p. 33.
2. Ibid.
3. Francine Ringold, "A Conversation With Paul Scott," *Nimrod*, 21,
no. 1 (1976), 18.
4. Benny Green, "Ironist," *Spectator*, March 11, 1978. p. 23.
5. Ibid.
6. Frank MacShane, *The Life of Raymond Chandler* (New York, 1976),
p. 95.
7. Letter, London, October 16, 1975. All references to letters are to
those addressed to the author of this study unless otherwise indicated.
8. *The Corrida at San Feliu* (New York, 1964), p. 17.
9. Letter, London, March 2, 1977.
10. John F. Baker, "Paul Scott," *Publishers Weekly*, September 15, 1975,
p. 6.
11. Mary Stocks, ed., *Essays by Divers Hands* (London, 1970), p. 113.
12. Roland Gant, "Paul Scott: An Obituary," *Bookseller*, March 11, 1978,
gives an account of Scott's involvement with this publishing venture. p. 12.
13. *Essays by Divers Hands*, p. 125. The Indian contribution to the growth
and prosperity of the English middle class is a recurring theme in the novels of
Scott. In an interview with the *London Times* (October 20, 1975), Scott
stated, "You see English faces that are well-nourished faces, faces with brains
inside their skulls, and they are as they are because we had an empire." Guy
Perron in *A Dvision of the Spoils* echoes the very same words (p. 103).
14. H. R. F. Keating, "Last Days of the Raj," *Country Life*, May 25, 1975,
p. 76, commenting on the use of India as a laboratory for English ideas notes,
"In the not so distant past [Scott] writes about, India was nothing less than
the great testing ground of all that was the British attitude to living. Even of
all that Western man stood for, since (let us admit it, though it is
unfashionable) not all that long ago the British attitude was the leading point
of Western civilization."
15. *Publishers Weekly*, p. 16. Of this financial backing by his publishers
Scott noted, "I've been lucky with my publishers," and as for the no strings
attached to the India trip to charge his batteries, "after all there might turn
out to be no batteries!"

16. *The Jewel in the Crown* is dedicated to Dorothy Ganapathy, one of the Indian families Scott stayed with.

17. Scott reviewed mystery fiction and later general fiction and nonfiction books for *London Times*. Since book reviews were anonymous until 1967, and because of lack of any indexing, it is not possible to list even some of them. In recent years Scott was a regular reviewer for *Country Life* (twice a month). Some of his reviews which have a bearing on this study have been included in the bibliography section.

18. Letter, London, January 8, 1978. "The one-volume *Quartet* sold its first printing but a reprint is just about ready. *Staying On* has reprinted twice and over Christmas crept back into the S/Times best seller chart of Top Ten, at Number 10. It has survived the New Year and come in today again in No. 9. So I am very content."

19. Benny Green, "The Ironist."

20. T. S. Eliot, *The Complete Poems and Plays 1909–1950* (New York, 1952), p. 129. Scott concluded his lecture "India: A Post Forsterian View" read to the Royal Society of Literature (December 5, 1968) by quoting the entire concluding passage from *East Coker*. See *Essays by Divers Hands*, p. 131–32.

Chapter Two

1. "I thought I had destroyed all copies of this poem," Scott remarked in the August 25, 1976, interview with the author of this study. All references to interviews will be to this interview unless otherwise indicated.

2. Peter B. Scott (letter, London, May 14, 1978) gives the following account of the genesis of the poem: "Paul accompanied me to Charing Cross Station, where I had to catch a train for somewhere in the South of England. Having some time to spare, we went into the buffet for coffee. On returning home Paul wrote the poem and sent me the typescript a few days later."

3. A typescript of *Sahibs and Memsahibs* is in the Paul Scott Collection at the Humanities Research Center, University of Texas, Austin.

4. Francine Ringold, pp. 24–25.

5. August 25, 1976, interview.

6. Ibid.

7. Caroline Moorehead, "Novelist Paul Scott," *London Times*, October 20, 1975, p. 8.

8. *Essays by Divers Hands*, p. 120. Scott's characters are workers. He believed in the importance of work. "There are two ways of looking at this obsession. In the obvious way, it seems to mean that the relationship between a man and his work is an emotional one and seen as at least as important and fascinating a subject for a writer of fiction as, let us say, the same man's sex life" (p. 121). Daniel J. Levinson, *The Seasons of a Man's Life* (New York, 1978), supports Scott's emphasis on the relationship between a man and his work when he writes, "A man's work is the primary lease for his life in society.

Through it he is 'plugged into' an occupational structure and a cultural class and social matrix. Work is also of great psychological importance; it is a vehicle for the fulfillment or negation of central aspects of the self."

9. *Publishers Weekly*, p. 16.

10. Letter, London, August 2, 1976.

11. Phillip Knightley, "Paul Scott: 1920–1978," *Sunday Times* (London), March 5, 1978, p. 10.

Chapter Three

1. *Essays by Divers Hands*, p. 120.

2. August 25, 1976, interview.

3. Anthony Burgess, *The Novel Now: A Guide to Contemporary Fiction* (New York, 1967), p. 157.

Chapter Four

1. *The Novel Now*, p. 157.

2. Maia W. Rodman, "*The Corrida at San Feliu*," *Saturday Review of Literature*, January 9, 1965, p. 48.

3. August 25, 1976, interview.

4. Telephone conversation, December 20, 1976.

5. Orville Prescott, "Brilliance Obscured by Ambiguity," *New York Times*, November 20, 1964. p. 18.

6. Ernest Buckler, "*The Corrida at San Feliu*," *New York Times Book Review*, November 1, 1964, p. 28.

7. Maia W. Rodman, p. 48.

8. *The Corrida at San Feliu*, p. 277.

9. *New Statesman*, August 28, 1964, p. 14.

10. Benny Green, "The Ironist."

11. Maia W. Rodman, p. 48.

12. August 25, 1976, interview. Scott finds his feelings for "words" best expressed in the opening lines of the concluding stanza of *East Coker*:

> Trying to learn to use words, and every attempt
> Is a wholly new start, and a different kind of failure
> Because one has only learnt to get the better of words
> For the one no longer has to say, or the way in which
> one is no longer disposed to say it. (p. 128)

13. Ibid.

14. Benny Green.

Chapter Five

1. *Essays by Divers Hands*, p. 120.

2. Ibid.

3. Maurice Richardson, "The Chinese Love Pavilion," *New Statesman*, October 8, 1960, p. 18.

4. *Essays by Divers Hands*, p. 120.

5. Ibid.

Chapter Six

1. Webster Schott, "Britons and Indians on the edge," *New York Times Book Review*, October 12, 1975, p. 33.

2. *John Kenneth Galbraith Introduces India*, ed. Frank Moraes and Edward Howe (London, 1974), p. 72.

3. The four volumes of *The Raj Quartet* will be cited in the text as *J, S, T,* and *D* respectively.

4. *Suttee*: the old Indian custom of burning a widow along with her dead husband on the funeral pyre. It was officially outlawed in the latter part of the nineteenth century during the viceroyalty of Lord William Bentinck.

5. The Catholic nun, Mother Theresa of Calcutta, inspired some aspects of Sister Ludmila's character. Scott had not met her. Malcolm Muggeridge's *Something Beautiful for God* is a study of her life and work.

6. Dyer is the one historical personality whose shadow looms in the background throughout *The Raj Quartet*. While Reid is cast in Dyer's mold, Bronowski comments that Dyer was a man who stubbornly held to the belief that he had been absolutely right and implies a similarity with Merrick (*D*, 156). An Indian doctor, Habibullah (whom Merrick admires), offers the theory that Dyer opened fire on unarmed Indians because of chronic amoebic infection. Perron lends credence to this view when he says that Dyer died of arterial sclerosis, a slow disease which might have affected his judgment. Dyer was born in India but sent back to England—in many ways a real banishment.

7. Francine Schneider Weinbaum, *Aspiration and Betrayal in Paul Scott's The Raj Quartet* (Ph. D. diss., University of Illinois, Urbana, 1977), p. 9. Weinbaum notes that Scott has "unsentimentally adapted Thackeray's *Vanity Fair* theme of war-loss, pregnant-wife, insanity," in Susan's story.

8. In selecting the Pathan as Merrick's servant-spy-aide, Scott strikes the right note. Homosexuality and bisexuality are accepted as facts of life by the Pathans. One of their proverbs is, "A woman to bear children, a boy for making love." One of their famous songs opens with the lament, "There is a boy across the river with a bottom like a peach, but alas I cannot swim." The Pathan outfit, which Merrick liked to wear, with its billowy harem plants and sash, and the shirt with billowy sleeves is as close to a drag outfit as any. John Masters, *Bugles and a Tiger* (New York, 1956), also notes the sexual preferences of Pathans. p. 192.

9. Webster Schott, p. 34.

10. J. G. Farrell, Review of *A Division of the Spoils*, *Times Literary Supplement*, May 23, 1975, p. 555.

Chapter Seven

1. Paul Scott, "Author's Thanks and Acknowledgements," *The Raj Quartet* (New York, 1976), p. 599.

2. *Essays by Divers Hands,* p. 116–17.

3. Ibid., p. 116.

4. Charles Allen and Michael Mason, ed., *Plain Tales From the Raj* (London, 1975), p. 216. Claude Auchinleck, field marshal and supreme commander of Southeast Asia in 1947, is quoted as saying, "The English never cared about India. They just used it." The same opinion is expressed by Robin White in *The Jewel in the Crown,* p. 317.

5. MAK writes a short letter to Mahatma Gandhi (*T*, 392); Sayed tells his father that he knew Shah Nawaz Khan of the INA slightly (*D*, 413); Barbie mentions that Edwina Crane knew Marcella Sherwood (*T*, 58); but there is not a single instance of an encounter between a character of Scott's imagination and a historical personality in the pages of *The Raj Quartet.*

6. Jean G. Zorn, "Talk with Paul Scott," *New York Times Book Review,* August 21, 1977, p. 37. Scott describes the locale of his imagined Mayapore, "If we split up the map of India, pull it apart just enough, to drive a wedge midway between Delhi and Calcutta, there the province would be." As for the perennial Smith's Hotel, "there is a version of it in every town" just as there is one in just about every novel of Scott's set in India.

7. Scott is so meticulous in his efforts to create a world of his own that he spells *his* state of Mirat differently from the real state of Meerut. To reenforce this point, when he describes Colin's arrival in India, he does so in the historical Meerut (*J*, 259), and not in the imaginative Mirat of Bronowski and the Nawab.

8. Max Beloff, "The End of the Raj: Paul Scott's Novels as History," *Encounter,* May, 1976, pp. 65–70.

9. Francis G. Hutchins, *The Illusion of Permanence: British Imperialism in India* (Princeton, 1967), p. 216.

10. Phillip Knightley, "Imperial Triumph," *Sunday Times* (London), May 4, 1975. p. 12.

11. Roger Beaumont, *The Sword of the Raj* (New York, 1977); the comments appear on the inside of the front jacket cover.

12. Phillip Knightley.

13. Letter from Mohan Singh, New Delhi, November 3, 1976. Singh comments on the accuracy of Scott's facts and descriptions concerning the INA. He particularly selects the second part of *The Towers of Silence* titled "A Question of Loyalty," for its authenticity of facts and their imaginative use.

14. Max Beloff, p. 70.

15. Nigel Nicolson, *Mary Curzon* (New York, 1977), p. 31.

16. August 25, 1976, interview.

Chapter Eight

1. Mrs. Turton, the collector's wife in E. M. Forster's *A Passage to India* (New York, 1924), represents the insularity and the clannish banding together of the English in India. She tells Adela Quested, a newcomer to India and with the zest for wanting to know about India like Daphne, "You're superior to everyone in India" (p. 42).

2. Maud Diver, *The English Woman in India* (London, 1909), wrote, "Englishmen and women in India are, as it were, members of one great family, aliens under one sky," and thus popularized one of the popular phrases of Raj days.

3. The solidarity the British had fanatically pursued during the Raj begins to come apart with the departure of the Raj. The British had kept the Indian out of their railway compartments. On the last train out of Mirat, Mrs. Grace wants to keep the Peabodys out! "Among themselves there emerges this dissension. The old solidarity has gone because the need for it has gone" (*D*, 554), Perron notes.

4. *Plain Tales from the Raj*, p. 90.

5. George Orwell, *Burmese Days* (New York, 1950), p. 9.

6. *Plain Tales from the Raj*, p. 17.

7. Ibid., p. 101.

8. Mohan Singh, *Soldiers' Contribution to Indian Independence: The Epic of the Indian National Army* (New Delhi, 1974), pp. 33–39. Singh points out the hierarchical caste system that existed within the British Indian Army; the low salaries the Indian officers received for the same job done by British officers; and the abolition of such distinctions by the Japanese in the early stages to win support of Indian soldiers.

9. Weinbaum, p. 130. It must also be noted that India with its own caste and class distinctions seemed like home for the English.

10. *Plain Tales from the Raj*, p. 37.

11. Lucy Tusker, even after the Raj's disappearance, still clings to residues of her racial prejudice. In *Staying On* (172–76) she has quite a time making up her mind whether to invite Susy Williams, a lady of mixed blood, to her house for dinner.

12. Kumar notices that his invisibility to the English begins even on the ship bringing him to India. The English, who had been friendly with him, changed "once past Suez" and formed their own circles of Turtonism and kept him out (*J*, 240).

13. *Plain Tales from the Raj*, p. 90. Eugene Pierce, a survivor from the days of the Raj, writes, "There was a very strong color bar. Conditions in those days strongly resembled present conditions in South Africa, with this difference that while in South Africa it is imposed by the government, in India it was accepted by mutual arrangement and tacit consensus."

14. Robin White's experiences in a remote Indian village, and his gradual breakthrough from the shell of Turtonism as a result of the compassionate

nursing by a motherly looking Indian woman, who gave him back his humanity (*J*, 324), has a parallel in Scott's own personal experience which he mentions in *Essays by Divers Hands*, p. 129.

Chapter Nine

1. Francine Ringold, p. 16.
2. David Holloway, "Requiem for India," *Daily Telegraph* (London), May 8, 1975, p. 9.
3. Kurosawa's film was also the basis for an American version, *Outrage*, with Paul Newman, Claire Bloom, and Edward G. Robinson. In both films the man is forced to become an eyewitness of the rape of his wife. Daphne, in her journal, writes of the manner in which Kumar had been forced to watch what was happening to her (*J*, 407).
4. Francine Ringold, p. 22.
5. Paul Scott, "A Smiling Villain [review of William Trevor's *Children of Dynmouth*]," *Country Life*, July 1, 1975, p. 65.
6. David Holloway.
7. Scott has stated on several occasions (August 25, 1976, interview) that he had no grand design for his four volumes. "I am not good at keeping journals, not even good at keeping notes. Besides, I do not believe in grandiose plans." Similar views are expressed in his interview with John F. Baker in *Publishers Weekly*, p. 16. In the August 25 interview he stated, "As I concluded *A Division of the Spoils*, I had this horrid idea that there was a fifth volume!"
8. Jean G. Zorn, p. 37.
9. August 25, 1976, interview.
10. Frank Giles, "Real Rubies for the Raj," *Sunday Times* (London), December 4, 1977, p. 8
11. Benny Green, "Lost Jewel," *Spectator*, July 23, 1977, p. 21.
12. Frank Giles.
13. Benny Green, "Ironist."
14. Theodore M. O'Leary, "Wide Recognition Must Come to Sequence on India," *Kansas City Star*, August 10, 1975, p. 18.

Chapter Ten

1. Interview with John Willey, New York, November 19, 1975.
2. Frank Giles.
3. Telephone conversation, December 18, 1977.
4. Malcolm Muggeridge, Review of *Staying On*, *New York Times Book Review*, August 21, 1977, p. 36.
5. Tusker gets his nickname because he belongs to the Mahwars regiment, their insignia being the tusks of an elephant. He is the only one to have this nickname.

6. Frank Giles.

7. Paul Scott, "Women in Love [review of *How I became a Holy Mother and Other Stories by Ruth Prawer Jhabvala*]," *Country Life*, July 15, 1976, p. 185.

Chapter Eleven

1. Anthony Burgess, "On Lengthy Matters," *New York Times Book Review*, December 14, 1975, p. 39.

2. David Pryce Jones, review of *A Division of the Spoils*, London *Times*, May 8, 1975, p. 16.

3. Webster Schott, p. 34.

4. Peter Green, "Casting off the Whiteman's Burden," *Book World* (*Washington Post*), August 10, 1975, p. 19.

5. *The Question of Henry James*, p. 62.

6. Ibid., p. 85.

7. Wilfred S. Dowden, *Joseph Conrad: The Imaged Style* (Nashville, 1970), p. 3.

8. Ibid., p. 9.

9. Richard A. Cassell, *Ford Madox Ford: A Study of His Novels*, (Baltimore, 1962), p. 203.

10. James Sheppard, review of *A Division of the Spoils, Time*, September 8, 1975, p. 69.

11. *Ford Madox Ford*, p. 214.

12. Letter, London, January 8, 1978.

13. Graham Greene makes extensive use of diaries, journals, and letters, as parts of his narrative technique. In *The Heart of the Matter* (New York, 1948), Scobie's diary and his letters to Helen and Louise keeps the flow of narrative. In *The End of the Affair* (New York, 1961), an entire section is devoted to Sarah's journal. The following styles are worth comparing: "If Louise had stayed I should never have loved Helen; I would never have been black-mailed by Yusef, never have committed that act of despair" (*The Heart of the Matter*, p. 253); "No Lindsey on the *maidan* that day, no drinking bout with young Vidyasagar and friends; no wandering on to waste-ground, no stretcher-barriers, no Sister Ludmila, no Sanctuary" (*D*, 301); "You plan to fight in Spain, and then before you know the tickets are taken for you, the introductions are pressed into your hand, somebody has come to see you off" (*The End of the Affair*, p. 323;) "My Sabbatical year was planned for me from the moment I opened my mouth; telephones rang, cables were sent, seats reserved on jet aircraft which flew God knew how many thousand feet" (*Birds of Paradise*, 16).

14. Peter Green, "Casting off the Whiteman's Burden."

15. Phillip Knightley, "Imperial Triumph," p. 12.

16. Max Beloff, p. 70.

17. H. R. F. Keating, "The Last Days of the Raj," p. 75.

18. Benny Green, "Lost Jewel," p. 21.

Selected Bibliography

PRIMARY SOURCES

1. Novels

Johnnie Sahib. London: Eyre and Spottiswoode, 1952.
The Alien Sky. London: Eyre and Spottiswoode, 1953. Published in U.S. as *Six Days in Marapore* (New York: Doubleday, 1953).
A Male Child. London: Eyre and Spottiswoode, 1956; New York: E. P. Dutton, 1957.
A Mark of the Warrior. London: Eyre and Spottiswoode, 1958; New York: William Morrow, 1958.
The Chinese Love Pavilion. London: Eyre and Spottiswoode, 1960. Published in U.S. as *The Love Pavilion* (New York: William Morrow, 1960).
The Birds of Paradise. London: Eyre and Spottiswoode, 1962; New York: William Morrow, 1962.
The Bender: Pictures from an Exhibition of Middle Class Portraits. London: Martin Secker and Warburg, 1963. Published in U.S. as *The Bender* (New York: William Morrow, 1963).
The Corrida at San Feliu. London: Martin Secker and Warburg, 1964; New York: William Morrow, 1964.
The Jewel in the Crown. London: William Heinemann, 1964; New York: William Morrow and Co., 1966.
The Day of the Scorpion. London: William Heinemann, 1968; New York: William Morrow, 1968.
The Towers of Silence. London: William Heinemann, 1971; New York: William Morrow, 1972.
The Division of the Spoils. London: William Heinemann, 1975. New York: William Morrow, 1975.
The Raj Quartet (One-Volume Edition). London: William Heinemann, 1976. New York: William Morrow, 1976.
Staying On. London: William Heinemann, 1977; New York: William Morrow, 1977.

2. Poetry

I, Gerontius—A Trilogy: The Creation—The Dream—The Cross. Resurgam Younger Poets Series, no. 5. London: Favil Press, 1940.

157

"Charing Cross Station." An Unpublished Poem. Copy with Peter Scott, London. July 28, 1941.

3. Plays (in manuscript at Humanities Research Center, University of Texas at Austin)

"Pillars of Salt." 1948.
"Lines of Communication." 1953.
"Sahibs and Memsahibs." 1955.

4. Essays

India: A Post-Forsterian View, Essays by Divers Hands, Ed. Mary Stocks. The Royal Society of Literature, New Series, Vol. XXXVI, London: Oxford University Press, 1970. Address delivered by Paul Scott to The Royal Society of Literature, London, December 5, 1968.
The Raj, John Kenneth Galbraith Introduces India, Ed. Frank Moraes and Edward Howe, London, Andre Deutsch, 1974.

5. Letters to K. Bhaskara Rao with the author of this study, University of Nevada, Reno.

London, September 15, 1966; London, October 16, 1975; London, August 2, 1976; London, March 14, 1976; University of Tulsa, Tulsa, Oklahoma, September 19, 1976; University of Tulsa, October 29, 1976; London, March 2, 1977; London, January 8, 1978.

6. Book Reviews

"The Continent of Circe by Nirad C. Chaudhuri." *Times Literary Supplement,* December 2, 1965, p. 1093.
"Gandhi by Geoffrey Ashe." *Times Literary Supplement,* April 11, 1968, p. 368.
"The Break-up of British India by Pandy" and "The Great Divide by Hodson." *Times Literary Supplement,* October 30, 1969, pp. 1257–58.
"George Eliot, The Emergent Self by Ruby V. Redinger." *Country Life,* March 11, 1976, p. 642.
"On a Shoestring to Coorg: An Experience of South India by Dervla Murphy." *Country Life,* April 8, 1976, pp. 923–24.
"The Children of Dynmouth by William Trevor" and "The Life of Raymond Chandler by Frank MacShane." *Country Life,* July 1, 1976, pp. 65–66.
"How I became a Holy Mother and other Stories by Ruth Prawer Jhabvala." *Country Life,* July 15, 1976, p. 185.

SECONDARY SOURCES

1. Biography and Criticism

BAKER, JOHN F. "Paul Scott." *Publishers Weekly*, September 15, 1975, pp. 6–7. Based on an interview with Paul Scott in New York. Of this Paul wrote to the author of this study in a letter (October 16, 1975): "The man who interviewed me in New York for the *Publishers Weekly* got so many things wrong. A nice fellow though. English too!"

BELOFF, MAX. "The End of the Raj: Paul Scott's Novels as History." *Encounter*, 272 (May, 1976), 65–70. A thoughtful article that explores the relationship between the novelist and historian, concluding that "Novels are an historical source that we are only now beginning to exploit."

BURGESS, ANTHONY. *The Novel Now: A Guide to Contemporary Fiction.* New York: Norton, 1967. Contains a short paragraph on Paul Scott in the chapter "Exports and Imports." References, however, are to Scott's earlier novels.

BURJORJEE, D. M. "*The Raj Quartet*: A Literary Event." *The New Quarterly*, 2, no. 2 (1977), 121–28. A review of the one volume edition of *The Quartet* by an Indian scholar whose study on *The Fiction of Anglo India* is in progress.

GILES, FRANK. "Real Rubies of the Raj." *Sunday Times* (London), December 4, 1977, p. 8. A brief but perceptive article written on hearing "Paul Scott now intends to give up writing about India," which statement, says Giles, is like hearing that "the Rothschild family will make no more vintage wines from their Lafite Vineyards." Of this article Paul Scott wrote to the author of this study in a letter (January 8, 1978): "This was a pleasant extra bonus, and certainly had its impact on pre-Christmas sales." The sales referring to *Staying On* and the one-volume edition of *The Raj Quartet*.

KEATING, H. R. F. "Last Days of the Raj [review of *A Division of the Spoils*]." *Country Life*, June, 1975, pp. 75–77. A significant review by a writer who himself has written about India in the creation of Ganesh Ghote, an Indian detective in the Ghote series. Keating points out the Proustian technique of Scott.

MOORHEAD, CAROLINE. "Getting Engrossed in the Death Throes of The Raj." *London Times*, October 20, 1975, pp. 8–11. Paul Scott notes several factual errors in the profile in a letter written to John Willey (October 22, 1975), his Editor at William Morrow and Co., New York, but adds "They are very very minor points and I thought she did a fine job."

MUGGERIDGE, MALCOLM. Review of *Staying On, New York Times*, August 21, 1977. A significant review by a former "Colonialist" who spent time in India during the heyday of the British Raj.

PARRY, BENITA. "Paul Scott's Raj." *South Asian Review*, (July-October 1975). Vol. VIII. No. 3, pp. 359–365. Parry's contention in this essay is that the symbol of the rape Scott uses is too weak to carry the entire epic story of the Raj's decline in India.

PRICE, R. G. G. "New Fiction." *Punch*, September 4, 1968, p. 21. In reviewing Paul Scott's *The Day of the Scorpion* (vol. 2 of *The Raj Quartet*), Price notes the Tolstoyan sweep and scope of Paul Scott's canvas and evaluates Scott as "One of the half dozen best living English novelists, to put it moderately."

RINGOLD, FRANCINE. "A Conversation with Paul Scott." *Nimrod*, 21, no. 1 (1976), 16–32. Interview conducted during Paul Scott's writer-in-residence period at the University of Tulsa. Contains incisive observations on the craft of writing as well as not so complimentary remarks on experimental writers.

WEINBAUM, FRANCINE SCHNEIDER. "Aspiration and Betrayal in Paul Scott's The Raj Quartet." Ann Arbor, Michigan: Xerox University Microfilms, 1976. A doctoral dissertation for the University of Illinois, Urbana-Champaign.

ZORN, G. JEAN. "Talk with Paul Scott." *New York Times Book Review*, August 21, 1977, p. 31. Written after the publication of Paul Scott's last novel *Staying On*.

2. Background

ALLEN, CHARLES, ed. *Plain Tales from the Raj: Images of British India in The Twentieth Century.* Introduction by Philip Mason. London: Andre Deutsch and B.B.C., 1975. The volume records the memories of British men and women who served the Raj during the last fifty years and is an indispensable volume in understanding the "atmosphere" of the British Raj. The volume is liberally illustrated with rare photographs and pages drawn from Army and Navy store catalogs.

———. *Raj: A Scrapbook of British India, 1877–1947.* New York: St. Martin's Press, 1978. With effective textual brevity and more than 200 photographs and illustrations taken from catalogs, scrapbooks, and official papers, the volume presents the power and grandeur of the British Raj in India during its heyday.

ALLEN, WALTER. *The English Novel.* New York: E. P. Dutton, 1954. A critical work admired by Paul Scott. Allen's definition of the novel as an extended metaphor for the novelist's personal view of life was acceptable to Scott.

BEAUMONT, ROGER. *The Sword of the Raj: The British Indian Army 1747–1947.* New York: Bobbs-Merrill, 1977. A nostalgic and pro-British study. Extensive quotes from British officers who served in the Indian Army provide valuable insights into the life of the British Raj.

BHARATHI, AGHENANDA. *The Ochre Robe: An Autobiography.* Garden City,

N. Y.: Doubleday, 1970. An excellent autobiography of the German-Viennese Catholic who, at age thirteen, became fascinated with India and everything Indian and took the name of Ramachandra, thus becoming Leopold Ramachandra Fischer. He joined the "Free India Legion" during the war to help India achieve her independence. Chapter 2, entitled *The Indian Legion*, gives a detailed yet succinct account of the formation of the Free India Legion (*Frei Hind*) as part of the German Army; Subhas Chandra Bose's fascination with Hitler and the German Army; the inner tensions between the Indian soldiers and the Germans with racist overtones; the reason why Indian POW's joined the Free India Legion; and comments on the attitude of Indian soldiers toward the British army. A good background to understanding the development of the Indian National Army in Europe, which is one of the themes of *The Raj Quartet*.

BOWLE, JOHN. *The Imperial Achievement: The Rise and Transformation of the British Empire*. Boston: Little, Brown, 1975. A passionate defense of the beneficial results of the British Empire.

CAMPBELL-JOHNSON, ALAN. *Mission with Mountbatten*. Bombay: Jaico Publishing House, 1951. The meticulously detailed day-by-day diary of the dissolution of the British Empire, maintained by a man who was the press attache to Lord Mountbatten, the last viceroy of India.

COLLINS, LARRY, and LAPIERRE, DOMINIQUE. *Freedom at Midnight*. New York: Simon and Schuster, 1975. A breezy, popular, easily readable account of Indian independence and its aftermath.

CORFIELD, CONRAD. *The Princely India I Knew: From Reading to Mountbatten*. Madras: Indo-British Historical Society, 1975. The author, the last head of the Political Department of the British Government of India, was involved in the confrontation between the Indian princes, the British Government, and the Indian Nationalists during the Imperial decline 1945–1947. He sympathized with the princes and could have been a model for Sir Robert Conway who in *The Birds of Paradise* and *A Division of the Spoils* counsels the Indian princes, unrealistically, to hold on without acceding either to India or Pakistan.

EDWARDS, MICHAEL. *The Last Years of British India*. Cleveland: World, 1963. A standard book on the subject.

———. *Glorious Sahibs: The Romantic as Empire Builder (1799–1838)*. New York: Taplinger, 1969. A fascinating study of the daily life of the British rulers in India.

FARRELL, J. C. *The Seige of Krishnapur*. New York: Harcourt Brace Jovanovich, 1973. A fictional recreation of the 1857 Sepoy Rebellion (some Indians refer to it as the first war of Indian Independence) which tears apart the Raj in India. The novel won the 1973 Booker Award.

FEIN, HELEN. *Imperial Crime and Punishment: The Massacre at Jallianwallah Bagh and British Judgement, 1919–1920*. Honolulu: University of Hawaii Press, 1977. An important sociopolitical study of an event that marked the beginning of the end of the British Raj in India. The impact of Jallianwallah Bagh is both implicitly and explicitly stressed by Paul Scott in *The Raj Quartet.*

FORSTER, EDWARD MORGAN. *A Passage to India.* New York: Harcourt, Brace, 1924. A classic novel about Indo-British relations.

————. *Hill of Devi.* New York: Harcourt, Brace, 1953. Forster's experiences in an Indian princely state.

————. *The Life to Come and Other Stories.* New York: Norton, 1972. Posthumously published collection. The stories explain in part why Forster never wrote fiction after "A Passage to India."

GANDHI, M. KARAMCHAND. *My Experiments with truth: An Autobiography.* Boston: Beacon Press, 1970. A direct honest autobiography of the man who more than anyone else was responsible for the break up of the British Raj.

GARDNER, BRIAN. *The East India Company.* New York: McCall, 1972. A well-documented account of the beginnings of the British Empire in India.

GUNTHER, JOHN. *Inside Asia.* New York: Harper and Brothers, 1939. Chapter 27, "The World of the Great Princes," discusses with insight, facts, and figures the strange, exotic, anachronistic world of Indian India or princely India—A world portrayed by Paul Scott in *The Birds of Paradise* and *A Division of the Spoils.*

HASTINGS, LIONEL ISMAY (LORD ISMAY). *The Memoirs.* New York: Viking, 1960. Life of the old Indian Army. Served as chief of staff to Lord Mountbatten during the dark days of the partition of the Indian subcontinent.

HOWE, SUSANNE. *Novels of Empire.* New York: Columbia University Press, 1949. An early study of the imperial themes in British fiction.

HUTCHINS, FRANCIS G. *India's Revolution: Gandhi and the Quit India Movement.* Cambridge: Harvard University Press, 1973. First published in 1971 under the title *Spontaneous Revolution: The Quit India Movement.* Excellent in providing the backdrop for a study of Paul Scott's *The Jewel in the Crown,* first volume of *The Raj Quartet.*

————. *The Illusion of Permanence: British Imperialism in India.* Princeton: Princeton University Press, 1967. A scholarly book outlining the reasons for the decline of the British in India.

JHABVALA, RUTH PRAWER. *Heat and Dust.* New York: Harper and Row, 1976. A short well-structured novel that "Visits" the British Raj which won the Booker Award in 1975.

KARL, FREDERICK R. *The Contemporary English Novel.* New York: Farrar, Strauss and Geroux, 1962. Contains a chapter on "George Orwell: The Whiteman's Burden!"

KIPLING, RUDYARD. *Plain Tales from the Hills.* Garden City, N.Y.: Doubleday, 1930. The collection of stories that brought fame to Kipling.

LORD, JOHN. *The Maharajahs.* New York: Random House, 1971. A delightfully entertaining account of the strange and exotic world of the Maharajahs.

MALGONKAR, MANOHAR. *The Princes.* New York: Viking, 1963. An excellent novel by an Indian author dealing with the dilemma faced by an Indian Maharajah and his son in India's new democracy. Deals with greater elaborateness the episode that Paul Scott touches on in *Six Days in Marapore* in the case of Jimmy, the Maharajah; and the case of Tradura and Krishi of Jundhapur in *The Birds of Paradise.*

MASON PHILIP. *A Matter of Honour: An Account of the Indian Army, its Officers and Men.* New York: Holt, Rinehart and Winston, 1974. An exhaustive study of the history of the Indian army as shaped by the British.

————. *Prospero's Magic: Some Thoughts on Class and Race.* London: Oxford University Press, 1962. A sociological study of the class and race relations betweeen colonial power and colonial people.

MENON, VAPAL PANGUNNI. *The Integration of Indian States.* Princeton: Princeton University Press, 1957. A valuable book by an Indian who handled the integration of Indian States. Paul Scott acknowledges the value of the book in his Author's Note to *The Birds of Paradise*: "I am also indebted to Mr. V. P. Menon's book The Integration of Indian States which I found invaluable as a political guide to some of the facts behind the fiction."

MOORHOUSE, GEOFFEREY. *Calcutta.* New York: Harcourt, Brace and Jovanovich, 1971. An impressive and fascinating account of the city that was the Second City in the British Empire.

MUGGERIDGE, MALCOLM. *Something Beautiful for God: Mother Theresa Calcutta.* New York: Harper and Row, 1971. Life of Sister Theresa is the prototype for Sister Ludmila in *The Jewel in the Crown.*

NEHRU, JAWAHARLAL. *My Autobiography.* New Delhi: Allied Publishers, 1962. Written for the most part when he was imprisoned by the British Raj, the volume presents the viewpoint of an Anglicized yet nationalistic Indian.

NICOLSON, NIGEL. *Mary Curzon.* New York: Harper and Row, 1977. Her reference to ignorance about India among the British, and observation that the British House (Parliament) emptied in haste when Indian affairs came up for discussion, corroborates Paul Scott's statement: "India was a great big bore to the British."

RAO, K. BHASKARA. *Rudyard Kipling's India.* Norman, Oklahoma: University of Oklahoma Press, 1967. An in-depth study of Kipling's India writings in relation to the reality of India.

REED, JOHN R. *Old School Ties: The Public Schools in British Literature.* Syracuse, N. Y.: Syracuse University Press, 1964. A convincing portrait of the close knit world of "School chums" and hence a good background book to Chillingborough mentioned in *The Raj Quartet.*

SINGH, MOHAN. *Soldier's Contribution to Indian Independence: The Epic of the Indian National Army.* New Delhi: Army Educational Stores, 1974. The autobiography of the Indian soldier who founded the Asian wing of the Indian National Army. Mohan Singh is one of the historical personalities referred to in *The Raj Quartet.*

TOYE, HUGH. *Subhas Chandra Bose.* Bombay: Jaico Publishing House, 1966. A good biography of the controversial Indian nationalist who inspired the formation of the Indian National Army.

WAKEFIELD, JOHN. *The Cloistered Elite: A Sociological Analysis of the English Public Boarding Schools.* New York: Praeger, 1969. Provides valuable insights into the ties that bind boys brought up in public schools.

WILSON, ANGUS. *The Strange Ride of Rudyard Kipling.* New York: Viking Press, 1978. A detailed study of Kipling by one of England's foremost novelists. Wilson analyzes each and every short story to reveal the craftsmanship of Kipling.

WILSON, EDMUND. *The Wound and the Bow: Seven Studies in Literature.* New York: Oxford University Press, 1947. The last study in the above volume is titled "Philoctetes: The Wound and the Bow" and is a concise and perceptive analysis of the Philoctetes legend, helpful in understanding the symbolism and psyche of Kumar, who calls himself Philoctetes when he writes for the local newspaper in *A Division of The Spoils.*

WORSICK, CLARK, and EMBREE, AINSLIE. *The Last Empire: Photography in British India, 1885–1911.* Preface by the Earl Mountbatten of Burma. Millerton, N. Y.: Aperture, 1976. A superb volume of photographs that reveal the military strength, the social complexity and the unimaginable grandeur of the Raj.

Index